DATE DUE

DE 1 '86 MY 27 '94		
MY 26 '87 MR 25 '95		
JE 1 '8		
AP 7 '88		
AP 25 '88		
MY 3 '89		
MY 26 '89		
OC 11 '90		
AP 23 '9		
SE 25 '93		
OC 9 '93		
OC 27 '9		

Youth Problems

Timely Reports to Keep
Journalists, Scholars and the Public
Abreast of Developing Issues, Events and Trends

Editorial Research Reports
Published by Congressional Quarterly Inc.
1414 22nd Street, N.W.
Washington, D.C. 20037

About the Cover

Cover illustration by Staff Artist Robert Redding.

Editor, Hoyt Gimlin
Managing Editor, Sandra Stencel
Editorial Assistants, Laurie De Maris, Nancy Blanpied

Production Manager, I. D. Fuller
Assistant Production Manager, Maceo Mayo

Library of Congress Cataloging in Publication Data
Main entry under title:

Youth problems.

"Editorial research reports."
Bibliography: p.
Includes index.
1. Youth — United States — Addresses, essays, lectures.
2. Juvenile delinquency — United States — Addresses, essays, lectures. 3. Social problems — Addresses, essays, lectures.
I. Editorial research reports.
HQ796.Y599 1982   362.7'96'0973   82-18222
ISBN 0-87187-244-7

Contents

Foreword

"Youth's the season made for joys," English poet John Gay wrote in 1728. But if Gay were writing in the 1980s, he might not make the same observation. Young people today are victims of social and cultural pressures that threaten to turn the halcyon days of youth into an ordeal.

Like their parents, children are struggling to cope with the effects of divorce, single parenthood, two-income families and an uncertain economy. The result, experts in child development say, is that many children are forced to assume adult responsibilities before they are ready.

"Children need time to grow, to learn, and to develop," child psychologist David Elkind wrote in *The Hurried Child: Growing Up Too Fast Too Soon* (1981). "To treat them differently from adults is not to discriminate against them but rather to recognize their special estate."

Evidence of stress among young people is not hard to find. Among those aged 14 to 24, suicide is the third leading cause of death, after accidents and homicides. Teen-age alcoholism and drug abuse are continuing problems. So is teen-age sex — over one million teen-agers become pregnant each year. More than two million juveniles were arrested for serious crimes last year.

Of course, most children make the transition to adulthood without permanent scars. But the pressures that drive some young people to aberrant or illicit behavior affect nearly all youngsters growing up in the United States. Today's young Americans may not remember childhood as the best years of their lives.

Sandra Stencel
Managing Editor

November 1982
Washington, D.C.

Pressures on Youth

by

**Robert Benenson
and Sandra Stencel**

**Aug. 13
1 9 8 2**

PRESSURES ON YOUTH

I T USED to be said that children were meant to be seen, not heard. That is hardly the case today. During the past year, the problems of America's children and teen-agers captured headlines in newspapers and magazines across the country. One news magazine ran cover stories on "troubled teen-agers" and "neglected kids." [1] *The Washington Post* printed a seven-part series on "Coming of Age in the 80s." [2] *The New York Times* ran a six-part series on juvenile crime. [3]

Discussion of youth problems is not exactly uncharted territory. In 1904, G. Stanley Hall wrote a two-volume work entitled *Adolescence: Its Psychology and Its Relations to Physiology, Anthropology, Sex, Crime, Religion and Education.* Hall described adolescence as the "best key to the nature of crime. It is essentially antisocial, selfishness, refusing to submit to the laws of altruism." Popular culture, even in supposedly more innocent times, often dealt with troubled youths. Films such as "Angels with Dirty Faces" and "Public Enemy" in the 1930s, "Boys' Town" in the 1940s, and "The Blackboard Jungle," "Rebel Without a Cause" and "West Side Story" in the 1950s and early 1960s are just a few examples.

While adolescence has always been considered a difficult period, today's teen-agers seem more troubled than those of previous generations. Concern is increasing as the percentage of young Americans involved in aberrant or illicit behavior grows. Statistics on drug and alcohol abuse, sexual activity, juvenile crime and suicide are way up. Not only are more youths doing these things, they are doing them earlier.

"Coming of age in America is inescapably stressful," said Dr. Herbert Pardes, director of the National Institute of Mental Health. "For even the sturdiest of adolescents and their parents, the passage from childhood to adulthood is rarely smooth; for those already on unsteady ground, the transition can become turbulent and painful." [4]

---

[1] Stanley N. Wellborn, "Troubled Teen-agers," *U.S. News & World Report*, Dec. 14, 1981, pp. 40-47, and Alvin P. Sanoff and Jeanne Thornton, "Our Neglected Kids," *U.S. News & World Report*, Aug. 9, 1982, pp. 54-58.
[2] *The Washington Post*, Dec. 27, 1981-Jan. 2, 1982.
[3] *The New York Times*, Feb. 28-March 5, 1982.
[4] Foreword to "Adolescence and Stress: Report of an NIMH Conference," National Institute of Mental Health, 1981, p. iii.

3

Drug Use Among Students*

	Class of 1976	Class of 1977	Class of 1978	Class of 1979	Class of 1980	Class of 1981
Alcohol	85.7%	87.0%	87.7%	88.1%	87.9%	87.0%
Marijuana	44.5	47.6	50.2	50.8	48.8	46.1
Stimulants	15.8	16.3	17.1	18.3	20.8	26.0
Cocaine	6.0	7.2	9.0	12.0	12.3	12.4
Methaqua-lone	4.7	5.2	4.9	5.9	7.2	7.6
Heroin	0.8	0.8	0.8	0.5	0.5	0.5

*Percent who used in last 12 months.
Source: National Institute on Drug Abuse.

According to a poll of 160,000 teen-agers conducted by Jane Norman and Myron Harris for their book *The Private Life of the American Teen-ager* (1982), almost 60 percent of those aged 16-18 and 33 percent of those aged 13-15 have had sexual intercourse. Increased sexual activity among young people has meant an increase in the number of illegitimate births. In 1979, the latest year for which complete statistics are available, 33 percent of babies born to white teen-agers and 83 percent of those born to black teen-agers were illegitimate. More than half a million children live with unmarried teen-age mothers.[5]

Drug use among youths soared during the 1970s and remains high. Alcohol is the drug students try most often and are most likely to continue to use. According to the Department of Health and Human Services, about 15 percent of the nation's 10th to 12th graders are problem drinkers or at substantial risk for developing a drinking problem. More than seven million young persons between the ages of 12 and 17 — 31 percent of that age group — report having tried marijuana more than once. Among high school seniors, over 60 percent have experimented with marijuana. While marijuana use appears to have leveled off, use of other drugs continues to climb *(see box, above)*.[6]

According to the Senate Subcommittee on Juvenile Justice, as many as one million children a year escape from their problems by running away from home. Many of these youngsters are victims of child abuse or neglect. They are also vulnerable to exploitation by pimps and pornographers. The National Committee for the Prevention of Child Abuse estimates that there may be as many as 600,000 child prostitutes in the nation.

Some desperate youths opt for the ultimate escape — suicide. Each year between 1,500 and 2,000 youths under age 20 are

[5] See "Sex Education," *E.R.R.*, 1981 Vol. II, pp. 633-652, and "Teen-age Pregnancy," *E.R.R.*, 1979 Vol. I, pp. 205-224.
[6] See "Marijuana Update," *E.R.R.*, 1982 Vol. I, pp. 105-124, and "Teen-age Drinking," *E.R.R.*, 1981 Vol. I, pp. 349-368.

listed as suicide victims.[7] While some youths take their frustrations out on themselves, many strike out at others. Young people traditionally have been responsible for a high percentage of crimes, but statistics indicate that youth crime is becoming more violent. According to the National Center for Juvenile Justice, juvenile arrests for violent crimes increased 41 percent from 1970 to 1979. The FBI reported that 1,237 persons under age 18 were arrested for murder in 1980.

Changing Environment and Expectations

Today's youth — defined as those under age 21 — were born after the post-World War II baby boom.[8] By past standards, they are a spoiled generation. They have grown up during a period when many people are affluent, most are comfortable and even the poor are cushioned against the severest devastations of poverty. They are the first generation for whom television, radio, the telephone, the automobile, even indoor plumbing, are virtually universal. On average, they have more leisure time, more money and more entertainment outlets, including today's omnipresent video games, than any previous generation.

But today's young people also were born and raised during a time of great political and social turmoil. Children as old as 18 were born after the assassination of President Kennedy. The Vietnam War, the 1960s youth revolt, the rising drug culture, soaring crime rates, inner-city riots, the civil rights movement, the women's liberation movement, Watergate, oil crises, the high-tech revolution, the arms race, television, runaway inflation and recession have all shaped the youth experience. So have the lifestyle changes of the past 20 years: rapidly rising divorce rates, single parenthood, two-income families, "the sexual revolution," overt homosexuality.

"Today's child has become the unwilling, unintended victim of overwhelming stress — the stress born of rapid, bewildering social change and constantly rising expectations," wrote child psychologist David Elkind. Adding to this stress, Elkind maintains, is the fact that society is forcing children to grow up too fast, to achieve too much in school and in sports, and to accept adult responsibilities before they are ready. "Children need time to grow, to learn, and to develop," he wrote in *The Hurried Child: Growing Up Too Fast Too Soon* (1981). "To treat them differently from adults is not to discriminate against them but rather to recognize their special estate."

---

[7] See "Youth Suicide," *E.R.R.*, 1981 Vol. I, pp. 429-448.
[8] The years most often given for the baby boom are 1946-61. In 1962, the U.S. fertility rate made its first sharp decline. However, the actual number of births remained high until 1965.

Some psychologists have criticized parents for using their children as tools in the battle to keep up with "the Joneses." In some ultra-competitive families children are judged not on the basis of their self-worth, but on their grades, clothes, extracurricular activities, college acceptances and career goals. While some youngsters thrive on the pressure, others are not up to it. "The abysmal experience of being average with super-smart parents puts enormous pressures on a teen-ager," said Dr. C. Gibson Dunn of the Springwood Psychiatric Center in Leesburg, Va. "The goals his parents set for him are often so far away that anything he can do will never measure up." [9]

Analysts also accuse some parents of having warped priorities. "The parents are saying, 'I really think it is important for you to achieve, and when you do I'll think about loving you,'" said Harvard University psychologist Tom Cottle. "It is contingency love. Love on the bonus plan. It should be love no matter what." [10]

Growing Importance of Peer Relations

Not only are parents expecting more from their children, so are other children. "There is a dictatorship of peers," one 15-year-old student told a reporter. "You have to have a tan, clothes, good grades." [11] Some psychologists believe that because of the increase in divorce and the growth of two-income families *(see p. 11)*, peer groups are exercising more influence on children. "Many adolescents are no longer nested in an intact family, so the stresses on them are bound to be greater," said Dr. T. Berry Brazelton, an associate professor of pediatrics at Harvard Medical School. "They are more at the mercy of peer pressure than they were 20 years ago." [12]

Others attribute the growing importance of peer relations to parents' changing attitudes toward child-rearing. Many adults have come to believe that they are entitled to pursue their own interests — even if it means devoting less time to their children and making fewer sacrifices for them. "Parents are caught in a crunch of conflicting values," said Edward Weaver, director of the American Public Welfare Association. "They value children, but they value other things as well, such as time for themselves, material goods, status and their careers. Given these conflicts, in a number of instances they neglect their children or don't give them a fair shake." [13]

[9] Quoted in *The Washington Post*, July 4, 1981.
[10] Quoted by Wellborn, *op. cit.*, p. 43.
[11] Quoted in *The Washington Post*, July 4, 1981.
[12] Quoted in "The Secret to Raising Healthy, Happy Children," *U.S. News & World Report*, Dec. 14, 1981, p. 46. Brazelton is also chief of the child-development division at Children's Hospital Medical Center in Boston.
[13] Quoted by Sanoff and Thornton, *op. cit.*, p. 54.

Anorexia Nervosa

A growing number of teen-agers are responding to the pressures and stresses of modern life by resorting to self-destructive behavior. One example is a psychological disorder known as anorexia nervosa, often called "the starvation disease" because its victims starve themselves to the point of serious illness or death. The National Association of Anorexia Nervosa and Associated Diseases (ANAD), based in Highland Park, Ill., estimates that there are at least 500,000 victims of anorexia nervosa in the United States. There may actually be many more, said a spokeswoman for the organization, because anorexia is still a "closet disease," like alcoholism used to be.

Approximately 90 percent of the victims are female, although ANAD reports a growing number of males seeking treatment. Although most of the literature on the subject has dealt with well-to-do, adolescent girls, ANAD sees the "white, teen-age, upper-middle-class anorexic" as something of a stereotype — anorexics have been found as old as 85 and as young as eight, and ANAD studies have found no socioeconomic correlation to the disease.

Anorexics are controlled by a compulsive desire or need to lose weight. Most begin with modest dieting goals, but once started, they lose control and either refuse to or find they cannot stop. Many stop eating altogether or subsist on a few hundred calories per day. Some take laxatives or diuretics. Others — perhaps as many as 50 percent according to ANAD — become bulimic, which means they purposely regurgitate anything they have eaten before it is absorbed.

The symptoms of advanced anorexia can be devastating. Many anorexics deteriorate to weights as low as 60-65 pounds. In the most severe cases, the body starts to feed on its own proteins, essentially eroding itself. Vital organs may collapse from lack of sufficient nutrients. Between 10-15 percent of anorexia nervosa victims die, most commonly from heart and kidney failure.

There are differing theories about the causes of anorexia nervosa. Some experts attribute the problem to our society's emphasis on beauty and thinness. Psychologists also report that many of their young female victims are afraid of growing up and having to become independent, and attempt to forestall womanhood, which they effectively do since the disease usually results in the cessation of menstruation and breast development. Other psychologists say that anorexia is a result of repressed anger at parents or a desperate need for attention.

Like other compulsions and addictions, anorexia nervosa is extremely difficult to treat. A big problem is that many anorexics deny there is anything wrong with them. It is not unusual for a near-skeletal anorexic to claim that she or he is getting fatter.

Some experts believe too much emphasis is placed on the negative aspects of peer group relations. "Young adults and adolescents will always be subject to peer pressure," Dr.

Judianne Densen-Gerber said in a recent interview. "You do that so you can form your own family and your own attachments."[14] According to Dr. John Hill of the Boys Town Center for the Study of Youth Development, "slavish peer conformity" occurs primarily "when children are driven out of the family through some form of permissive neglect or extreme authoritarianism." [15]

❊ New Concerns About Media's Influence

By the time the average child has graduated from high school, he or she will have spent 12,000 hours in the classroom and 18,000 hours watching television. The impact of television on children is a subject of much debate. Network executives insist there are no definitive studies indicating that television can be damaging to children. But the overwhelming majority of people responding to a recent poll (71 percent) agreed that violence on television produces aggressive behavior in children.[16]

Others are concerned about the relative lack of quality in children's programming and youngsters' increasing access to sexually explicit programs, including "R" and "X" rated movies shown on cable and subscription TV. David Elkind believes television contributes to the "hurried-child" syndrome."

> Young children are seeing more on television than their grandparents ever saw in a lifetime [he wrote]. By homogenizing age groups and appealing to the eighteen-to-forty-nine-year-old audience, television . . . treats even young children as grown-up, as part of the large "common" audience. Consequently, even young children seem quite sophisticated about the major issues of our time — drugs, violence, crime, divorce, single parenting, inflation and so on. . . . But much of this knowledge is largely verbal. Adults, however, are often taken in by this pseudosophistication and treat children as if they were as knowledgeable as they sound.[17]

Studies indicate that the average child watches more than 20,000 television commercials a year.[18] Many adults are worried about the impact that all this advertising is having on the minds and bodies of the nation's youngest consumers — and on the wallets of their parents. "Childhood at times seems to be nothing more than a succession of material wants and yearnings: to

---

[14] Densen-Gerber is the founder and head of Odyssey Institute in New York City. The institute was founded in 1966 as a drug rehabilitation center, but has since expanded its areas of interests to include various child welfare issues including child abuse, child pornography and prostitution and age of consent.
[15] Speaking at a conference on "Adolescence and Stress" sponsored by the National Institute of Mental Health in September 1980.
[16] Findings of "The Merit Report: A Public Opinion Survey" conducted June 8-13, 1982. "The Merit Report" is sponsored by Merit cigarettes.
[17] David Elkind, *The Hurried Child: Growing Up Too Fast Too Soon* (1981), p. 77.
[18] See E. Kaye, *The ACT Guide to Children's Television* (1979).

eat Big Macs, to play with Tonka trucks, to wear Underoos, to go camping with Barbie and Ken," Christopher Johnson wrote in *Today's Education.*[19]

Sexual overtones in recent ads for all sorts of kids' products, especially blue jeans, have prompted a rash of criticism. "What's disturbing about these commercials is that they open up a new frontier by portraying boys and girls in very sexual situations," said Kim Hays of Action for Children's Television (ACT). "We feel it's important for 12- and 13-year-olds to know about sex, but not the way advertisers present it."[20]

The most controversial jean ads feature teen-age actress and model Brooke Shields making what some regard as sexually enticing testimonials. "What comes between me and my Calvins (Calvin Klein jeans)?" Shields asked in one ad. "Nothing," came the reply. Viewers' complaints about her body language led the three major television networks to ban what one executive called "the more explicit commercials."

Many observers are concerned about the image of teen-age sexual precocity portrayed in such recent films as "Pretty Baby," "Endless Love," "Taxi Driver," "Foxes" and "The Blue Lagoon." Also objectionable to many child welfare advocates are rock music lyrics that, they say, glorify sex and drug use. "Permitting kids . . . to have as role models pop singers who sing about drugs is a disaster," said Dr. Densen-Gerber. Rep. Robert K. Dornan, R-Calif., recently introduced a bill in Congress that would require warning labels on record albums that he says contain hidden messages extolling satanic worship. A similar bill was introduced in the California Legislature.

Economic Pressures: Education and Jobs

Children were never entirely spared from economic troubles. Poverty has always severely affected the young. It was not until the early part of this century that child labor laws were passed to protect children from economic exploitation *(see box, p. 13).* But today, economic pressures are not limited to poor youths, but are being felt by middle-class and upper middle-class youngsters who were long sheltered from economic uncertainties. Probably the greatest worry of youths from all economic backgrounds is that they will be the first generation to be less well off than their parents.

"America has been built on the idea of upward mobility,"

---

[19] Christopher Johnson, "The Standardized Child," *Today's Education,* November-December 1981, p. 27.
[20] ACT, a Boston-based group of parents and educators founded in 1968, is the leader of the movement to restrict advertising on children's television programs and is responsible for many of the reforms in children's programming.

Today's youth may be less well off than their parents.

wrote Robert J. Samuelson, "but the current slump — actually the entire economic experience of the past decade — has raised the specter of downward mobility. Seditious though it sounds, it's an idea that is clearly troubling a lot of Americans." [21] Nearly 70 percent of those responding to a March 8, 1982, *Washington Post*-ABC News Survey thought they were better off than their parents, but only 43 percent thought their children would be in the same position.

One reason for this kind of pessimism is that today's youths were preceded into the job market by the 65 million members of the "baby boom." This group, which includes the parents of some of today's children, is the best educated and, despite the nation's recent economic problems, the most upwardly mobile generation in American history. And because of the size of the baby boom group, the generation following it may find the paths to success blocked by their elders. This problem may be partially offset by early training of young people in new, expanding technologies. But when many of today's youths reach their 30s and 40s, they may find the executive and managerial positions they seek already occupied.

The nation's economic retrenchment, the highly competitive job market, the decline of high-paying blue-collar jobs and the transition to a computer-and-technology oriented society have made a college education increasingly important. At the same time, higher education is becoming more difficult to attain. According to the National Center for Educational Statistics, tuition costs at public colleges rose an average of 66 percent

---

[21] Robert J. Samuelson, "Downward Mobility," *National Journal*, July 31, 1982, p. 1347.

from 1974-75 to 1981-82; private college tuition went up 89 percent. College loans are harder to obtain and are available only at high interest rates. Federal student aid programs have been trimmed by the Reagan administration *(see box, p. 16)*. Unless these economic conditions change, many more young people will have to defer their college education, start working younger and longer to save for college, go to college part-time while holding part- or full-time jobs, or forgo college altogether.

For those youths who do not obtain a higher education, especially those from poorer households, the changing economy is creating new pressures. Unskilled blue-collar jobs, a traditional outlet of opportunity for poor youths, are disappearing as factories close or workers are replaced by machines.[22] Even the part-time jobs where young people have gotten a start, such as in fast-food restaurants and supermarkets, are being competed for by hard-pressed adults. Youth unemployment in July was 24.1 percent; black youth unemployment was 49.7 percent.

Changes in the Family

WHILE today's youth may face special problems, adolescence has long been recognized as a period of development fraught with stressful aspects. Adolescence "is a period of extraordinary change, multiple conflicts and marked societal demands upon the individual for the successful completion of significant developmental tasks," wrote Dr. Norman Garmezy of the University of Minnesota. "On the side of change, there are the hormonal, physiological and somatic changes that are reflected in pubertal development.... Equally important psychological changes are spurred on by this rapid physical development.... As for conflict, this tends to be focused on parents as the most significant adults in the life of the adolescent." [23]

Intensifying the usual parent-child conflicts have been the extraordinary changes in family life in the past two decades.[24] A report issued by the National Center for Health Statistics in November 1980 projected that one of every two marriages in the United States will eventually end in divorce.[25] In 1981, according to the Census Bureau, there were over 1.2 million divorces in the United States. About 5.5 million children under age 18 were living with a divorced parent last year.

---

[22] See "America's Employment Outlook," *E.R.R.*, 1982 Vol. I, pp. 385-408 and "The Robot Revolution," *E.R.R.*, 1982 Vol. I, pp. 345-364.
[23] Overview to "Adolescence and Stress: Report of an NIMH Conference," *op. cit.*, p. 3.
[24] See "Changing American Family," *E.R.R.*, 1977 Vol. I, pp. 413-432.
[25] The report, "National Estimate of Marriage Dissolution and Survivorship," was written by Dr. James A. Weed, who is now with the U.S. Census Bureau.

Divorce can have serious psychological consequences for children and adolescents. Even when custody is not contested, parents often confuse children by competing for their loyalties. Aside from the obvious disruption of the normal family routine, divorce frequently threatens a child's sense of security because of the family's diminished economic circumstances or the child's fear of losing the remaining parent. Some children blame themselves for their parents' problems.

Divorce often thrusts children into roles for which they are not prepared. For instance, some divorced parents turn to their children for friendship. "I debrief with the kids when I get home from work the way I used to with my husband...," said one divorced mother. "I guess I tell them more than I ought to about my worries, but they might as well find out sooner or later that life can be complicated, unfair and infuriating." [26] Psychologist David Elkind is among those who believe parents should not put such burdens on their children. "Children are hurried into mature interpersonal relations because the parent is under stress and needs a confidant...," he wrote. "Unfortunately ... it is by no means clear that this is what the child needs." [27]

Implications of Women's Employment

One of the most significant changes in family lifestyles in recent years has been the increase in the number of working women. Over half of the adult female population is now in the labor force. According to the Bureau of Labor Statistics, over half of all children under age 18 have working mothers.[28] The Census Bureau reported July 29 that 45 percent of all mothers of preschool children were working in 1980, up fourfold from 1950.

The arrival of the two-paycheck family has been accompanied by a redefinition of family roles. As women contribute more to families' economic welfare, their husbands and children are expected to do more around the house. In many households, children are expected not only to do the dishes and clean their rooms, but to do the family grocery shopping, cook some of the meals and help care for younger children.

In the past the children of working mothers were usually cared for in the home by grandparents or other relatives. Today, however, 48.7 percent of the children of full-time working mothers are cared for in day-care centers or by babysitters who are not related to the child. For preschoolers, this figure is 62

[26] Quoted by Marie Winn in "What Became of Childhood Innocence?" *The New York Times Magazine,* Jan. 25, 1981, p. 16.
[27] Elkind, *op. cit.,* p. 42.
[28] Allyson Sherman Grossman, "More Than Half of All Children Have Working Mothers," *Monthly Labor Review,* February 1982, pp. 41-43.

Child Labor

The Reagan administration caused a flap July 16 when it announced proposed regulations concerning work rules for 14- and 15-year-olds. The regulations would broaden the hours and types of jobs that could be performed by children in this age group. Opposition from labor, parent, teacher and child protection groups resulted in the withdrawal of the proposed regulations pending further review.

Child labor has not been much of a national issue in recent years, but it certainly was one earlier in the century. Hundreds of thousands of children, many of them under age 10, performed dirty and often dangerous work in coal mines, glass factories, cigarette and textile mills and other industrial locations. A widespread movement evolved to protest child labor. Although a number of states passed child labor laws, similar efforts at the federal level were often thwarted. The Supreme Court ruled congressional child-labor laws unconstitutional in 1918 and 1922. In 1924, a constitutional amendment controlling child labor was passed by Congress, but was not ratified by enough states.

Finally, in 1938, Congress passed child labor regulations that stood up as part of the Fair Labor Standards Act. This law set 14 as the minimum age for non-manufacturing work outside of school hours, 16 for employment in interstate commerce during school hours, and 18 for hazardous occupations. Children aged 14 and 15 were not permitted to work after 7 p.m., were allowed to work only three days and 18 hours during the school week, and were barred from "dangerous" jobs such as operating and repairing power-driven kitchen implements, such as food slicers and grinders.

The changes that the Reagan administration is considering would affect these regulations. Children 14 and 15 would be allowed to work until 9 p.m. on school nights and until 10 p.m. on non-school nights. The work week would be expanded to four days and 24 hours, and the prohibition against certain types of work would be lifted. William Otter, the Department of Labor's wage and hour administrator, told the House Labor Standards Subcommittee July 28 that the new rules would "improve the employment opportunities of young workers without harming their health, well-being or opportunity for schooling." But Thomas Donahue, secretary-treasurer of the AFL-CIO, said that the regulations would "create a pool of cheap, part-time child labor, the beneficiaries of which would be the various industries that already have notorious records for violating and undercutting fair labor standards."

percent. Many parents find private day-care or babysitting arrangements unsatisfactory, unavailable or too expensive. Public day care is available only to a very small percentage of children. The result is that many children are left on their own all day or return to empty houses after school. There are an estimated 4-10 million of these so-called "latchkey" children.

For some youngsters, the "latchkey" experience provides valuable lessons in responsibility, caution and independence. But experts in child development say that being left alone for long periods can be harmful for many children. Professor Lynette Long of Loyola College in Baltimore said that almost all the latchkey children she interviewed for an upcoming book on the subject had frequent nightmares about someone breaking into their homes.[29] Police say latchkey children are particularly susceptible to attack or injury. The lack of adult company and guidance may also contribute to juvenile crime. For example, when a Portland, Ore., YMCA began a program for latchkey children, vandalism at three local schools fell from $12,000 to $200 in one year.

Severity of Child Abuse, Neglect Problem

Child abuse and neglect have always been around, but experts say the problem is on the rise. The American Humane Association (AHA) reported that there were 788,844 official reports of child maltreatment in 1980, involving an estimated 1.2 million children. This represented a 91 percent increase over 1976. Many other incidents were never reported.[30]

Some of the increase may be attributable to more accurate data-gathering efforts, but child abuse authorities say the increases are real. Dr. Ann H. Cohn, executive director of the National Committee for the Prevention of Child Abuse (NCPCA), told Editorial Research Reports that even in areas where advertising and public awareness about child abuse have been evident for a long time, child abuse statistics have shown a significant increase. "If you talk to protective service workers in every major city, there's been increasing numbers of really serious cases of child abuse, dramatic increases in the numbers of deaths due to child abuse," she said. According to the American Humane Association, 20 percent of child abuse victims suffer minor physical injury and 4 percent suffer major physical injury. NCPCA estimates that between 2,000 and 5,000 youngsters die each year as a result of child abuse.

Cohn believes there are two primary factors behind the recent increase in child abuse: (1) the nation's economic problems, which produce severe stress for many families and create the volatile atmosphere in which abuse can occur; and (2) the fact that many of the social, health and day-care services that were available to low-income families are being scaled back or eliminated by government budget cutting. "I think as we start to pull those supports away from families, we also will see increasing amounts of child abuse," Cohn said.

[29] Quoted by Stanley N. Wellborn in "When School Kids Come Home to an Empty House," *U.S. News & World Report*, Sept. 14, 1981, pp. 42-47.
[30] See "Violence in the Family," *E.R.R.*, 1979 Vol. I, pp. 305-324.

About 7 percent of reported child abuse victims, or approximately 84,000 youngsters, were sexually abused. "There seems little doubt that the incidence of sexual abuse committed against children is vastly higher than anyone would like to believe," stated an NCPCA pamphlet, "with the shocking possibility that the annual incidence could be in excess of 1,000,000." Cohn said that 90 percent of teen-age prostitutes claim to have been sexually abused as children.

Coping With the Problem

ALL THE attention given to youth problems in recent years has prompted a get-tough attitude among many adults. This is particularly true in the area of juvenile justice. "There is little doubt among juvenile justice experts — or legislators who specialize in the field — that a heightened public awareness of juvenile crime is creating pressures for a crackdown on what is seen as the softness and lenience of juvenile courts," Richard W. Foster wrote in a magazine published by the National Conference of State Legislatures in Denver, Colo.[31]

New York was one of the first states to enact special legislation to toughen treatment of juvenile offenders. A 1976 law required minimum sentences for youths judged to be responsible in juvenile courts for certain violent crimes. A 1978 law facilitated waivers of youthful offenders to adult courts for certain violent felonies. According to Foster, other states have followed the current trend in adult justice and set minimum or fixed sentences for juveniles convicted of crimes.

Parents themselves are sometimes resorting to tough measures to control unruly children. In 1980, professional youth counselors David and Phyllis York of Lansdale, Pa., founded the "Toughlove" movement, which advocates strict parental discipline. The Yorks developed this approach after their own daughter repeatedly got into trouble. The theory behind Toughlove is that forgiving or accepting the behavior of troublemaking children, no matter how well meaning, is often ineffective or counterproductive. "It's just old-time discipline, where parents run the home and there is cooperation among family members," said one member.[32]

[31] Richard W. Foster, "Juvenile Justice in the United States," *State Legislatures*, January 1982, p. 20.
[32] Quoted in *Time*, June 8, 1981.

Student Aid Reductions

When the Reagan administration came to office in 1981, federal aid to college students was one of those areas targeted for budget savings. Student aid had been one of the fastest growing federal programs. According to the Senate Budget Committee, federal spending on the guaranteed student loan (GSL) program grew by 82 percent between 1976 and 1981.

The major targets of White House and congressional budget cutters were the two largest student aid programs: the Pell grants (named after Sen. Claiborne Pell, D-R.I.), which in fiscal year 1981 provided 2.7 million mainly lower- and lower-middle-class students with an average of $838 in grants-in-aid, and the guaranteed student loan program, which provided interest subsidies to banks and guaranteed payments of loans to 3.5 million mainly middle-class students in fiscal year 1981. According to the Congressional Budget Office, cuts ordered in last year's budget reconciliation law will result in the reduction or elimination of guaranteed loans to families with incomes over $30,000. Pell Grants will be reduced by an average of $80. Approximately 650,000 students who had been receiving Social Security benefits as children of retired, disabled or deceased workers will have their benefits reduced by an average of $2,500 in 1983.

The 1983 budget proposal submitted by the president to Congress this year included further cuts in federal student aid. This time, though, the budget proposals were met with united and fierce opposition from education and student lobbies. On March 1, a National Student Lobby Day drew 5,000 students to Washington to demonstrate against the budget cuts and to lobby representatives and senators to vote against them.

The Senate Budget Committee reduced the proposed cuts, but Senate Republican leaders decided even this was too much, given the political pressure, and dropped the student aid cuts altogether. The Democratic-controlled House committees did likewise. When reconciliation instructions were sent to committees following the passage in June of the first budget resolution, no cuts were ordered in student aid programs.

A spokesman for Toughlove said there were about 600 chapters in 48 states, Canada, West Germany, Britain and Guam. Members act as a support group for other parents, sharing experiences and offering advice. Members are encouraged to set strict rules and to punish children if they misbehave or get into trouble. Less severe punishments might include removal of telephone and automobile privileges or curfews. If children continue to cause trouble within or outside the home, Toughlove parents may lock them out of the house, supplying them with the names of other members who have agreed to take them in until they agree to live by the family rules. If a problem becomes incorrigible, Toughlove encourages parents to instruct children to get professional help or move out. Toughlove also discourages parents from bailing their children out if they get into trouble with the police.

Some mental health experts have reservations about the Toughlove program. Dr. Lawrence A. Brain, a psychiatrist from Bethesda, Md., believes universal solutions can be dangerous when dealing with the individual, often delicate, psychological problems of a troubled youth. When dealing with children under age 18, he said, "structure must be set up in a flexible and compassionate way." [33] Many psychiatrists believe that except in extreme circumstances children should never be thrown out of the house. "The more disturbed the child is, the more cautious one should be about letting him go," said Dr. Toksoz B. Karasu, chairman of the American Psychiatric Association's Commission on Psychiatric Therapies.[34]

Attempts to Control Kids' Sexual Activity

Many adults, especially those who are politically conservative, are attempting to control children's sexual behavior. The Reagan administration is considering a regulation that would require federally funded family planning clinics to notify parents when children under age 18 are given birth control prescriptions. Supporters blame the easy availability of contraceptives for the rise in youth sexuality. Opponents say it will simply scare sexually active youths away from family planning clinics, resulting in more teen-age pregnancies.

Last year Congress authorized funding for a controversial teen-age sexuality program that its supporters hoped would help discourage sexual activity among teen-agers. The program, funded at $30 million a year for three years, continued an existing program that provided pregnant teen-agers with prenatal care and counseling. But it also provided funds for "preventive services," which were to be provided by maternity homes, YWCAs and others who operate programs for pregnant teen-agers. As originally drafted by Sen. Jeremiah Denton, R-Ala., the bill called for the promotion of teen-age "chastity" as a solution to "the problem of adolescent promiscuity," but that language was dropped.[35]

Teen-age sexuality was one of the issues discussed at a recent conference, Family Forum II, sponsored by the Moral Majority Foundation and other "New Right" groups. More than 500 adherents of the so-called "pro-family movement" attended the July 27-29 conference and heard such speakers as Dr. J. Craig Perry, special assistant on child and family issues to Sen. Orrin

---

[33] Quoted in *The Washington Times,* July 21, 1982.
[34] Quoted in *The New York Times,* May 14, 1982.
[35] See *1981 CQ Almanac,* pp. 487-488.

Teen-agers are more likely to make choices their parents like when they are not pushed to do so.

G. Hatch, R-Utah, and George Gilder, author of *Wealth and Poverty* (1980). Perry told the group that their tax dollars were paying for such things as "sex education programs that are in contradiction with the Bible" and "adolescent and family planning programs that say to children ... 'Your parents are old-fashioned and so we will explain sex to you and help you avoid having a baby.' "

A Different View of Adolescent Behavior

While some adults are concentrating on ways to control adolescent behavior, Dr. Richard Jessor, a University of Colorado psychologist, has suggested that such things as cigarette smoking, alcohol and drug use, sexual activity and physical aggressions may be part of normal adolescent development and play an important role in the process of transition to young adulthood. "The argument can be made that coming to terms with alcohol, drugs and sex has emerged as a new developmental task that all adolescents face as part of the normal process of growing up in contemporary American society," he said in a paper presented at the 10th annual Schering Symposium on Adolescence held during the annual American School Health Association convention last fall.[36] "Since problem behavior is ... unlikely to disappear," Jessor concluded, it is important to understand it and attempt to reduce its negative personal and social consequences.

[36] Excerpts from his remarks reprinted in *PTA Today*, May 1982, p. 23.

According to psychologists Robert and Jean Bayard, parents have to recognize that they cannot dictate their children's behavior. "In their love and concern for their children, parents often decide how the children should behave, and then push them to do so — to do their homework, to choose the 'right' sort of friends, and so on," they wrote. "Well meant as this may be, it nonetheless tends to lower teen-agers' self-esteem and make them unsure of their abilities to make their own decisions." Instead, they suggest that parents put the responsibility for the teen-ager's decisions squarely on his or her own shoulders. "This is not easy for many parents," they said, "but it can have powerful positive effects in improving the family situation. Paradoxically, teen-agers seem *more* likely to make choices their parents like when they are not pushed to do so."[37]

It is worth noting that most children make the transition to adulthood with few permanent scars. As reporter Dan Morgan noted in *The Washington Post:* "Statistics show 90 percent of high school students do not use drugs frequently; 94 percent do not drink alcohol every day; 97 percent have not used a knife or gun to get something from somebody else; 97 percent have never struck a teacher, and 85 percent of teen-age girls never get pregnant." [38] Apparently, most children do know what is in their best interests.

---

[37] Robert T. Bayard and Jean Bayard, "How To Deal With Your Acting-Up Teen-ager," *PTA Today,* May 1982, p. 22.
[38] *The Washington Post,* Dec. 27, 1981.

▼▼▼

Selected Bibliography

Books

Califano, Joseph A. Jr., *The 1982 Report on Drug Abuse and Alcoholism*, Warner, 1982.

Elkind, David, *The Hurried Child: Growing Up Too Fast Too Soon*, Addison-Wesley, 1981.

Keniston, Kenneth, *All Our Children: The American Family Under Pressure*, Harcourt Brace Jovanovich, 1977.

Offer, Daniel, Eric Ostrov and Kenneth I. Howard, *The Adolescent: A Psychological Self-Portrait*, Basic, 1981.

Articles

Cevoli, Cathy, "Is There Anything a 28-Year-Old Can Teach Her Teenage Sister (That She Doesn't Already Know)?" *Ms.*, February 1982.

Foster, Richard W., "Juvenile Justice in the States: Which Way Is It Heading?" *State Legislatures*, January 1982.

Grossman, Allyson Sherman, "More Than Half of All Children Have Working Mothers," *Monthly Labor Review*, February 1982.

Helgesen, Sally, "Theoretical Families," *Harper's*, January 1982.

Johnson, Christopher, "The Standardized Childhood," *Today's Education*, December 1981.

Long, Lynette and Thomas J. Long, "What To Do When The Children Are Home Alone," *Essence*, March 1982.

O'Roark, Mary Ann, "The Alarming Rise in Teenage Suicide," *McCall's*, January 1982.

Sanoff, Alvin P., et al., "Our Neglected Kids," *U.S. News & World Report*, Aug. 9, 1982.

Wellborn, Stanley N., "Troubled Teen-agers," *U.S. News & World Report*, Dec. 14, 1981.

— "When Kids Come Home To An Empty House," *U.S. News & World Report*, Sept. 14, 1981.

Reports and Studies

Editorial Research Reports: "Marijuana Update," 1982 Vol. I, p. 107; "Youth Suicide," 1981 Vol. I, p. 431; "Teen-age Drinking," 1981 Vol. I, p. 351; "Juvenile Justice," 1979 Vol. II, p. 543; "Violence in the Family," 1979 Vol. I, p. 307; "Teen-age Pregnancy," 1979 Vol. I, p. 205.

National Center for Juvenile Justice, "The Serious Juvenile Offender: The Scope of the Problem and the Response of Juvenile Courts," September 1981.

National Committee for Prevention of Child Abuse, "An Approach to Child Abuse," 1981.

National Institute of Mental Health, "Adolescence & Stress: Report of a NIMH Conference," 1981.

National Institute on Alcohol Abuse and Alcoholism, "Alcohol Topics In Brief," 1980.

National Institute on Drug Abuse, "Highlights from Student Drug Use in America 1975-1981," 1982.

Cover illustration by Staff Artist Cheryl Rowe;
photos p. 10 and p. 18 by Ken Heinen.

YOUTH SUICIDE

by

Jean Rosenblatt

June 12
1981

YOUTH SUICIDE

THIS YEAR more than 5,000 young Americans can be expected to kill themselves. Suicide has increasingly taken a heavier toll among the nation's youth, trailing only accidents and homicides as the leading cause of death for those between ages 15 and 24. Even younger children are sometimes unhappy enough to take their own lives; the National Center for Health Statistics reported almost 2,000 documented cases of suicide among children under 14 during a 13-year period ending in 1978, the latest year for which official figures are available.

Though official statistics are lacking for more recent years, mental health professionals do not discern any decline in the incidence of youth suicide. Some experts say that there are two to three suicides for every one recorded. The National Center for Health Statistics does not document suicide trends for children under 10, yet these children are believed to be committing suicide in increasing numbers. Also, many suicides are reported as accidents either to protect the families involved or because the coroner's office had no evidence of intentional death. For example, life-threatening risks that end in death are sometimes considered suicides in disguise, or "sneaky suicides."

Many more teen-agers attempt suicide than commit it. Dr. Michael Peck, director of youth services at the Suicide Prevention Center in Los Angeles, believes that as many as 50,000 young people may attempt suicide in the United States each year and about a million or more children have suicidal crises, thoughts and episodes. Peck's research suggests that "up to 10 percent of the youngsters in any public school classroom may be considered at some risk for suicide."[1]

Before the mid-1960s, suicide rates in the United States and most of the world increased with age, so that the lowest rates were among the young. But here and in several other advanced industrial nations, youth suicide rates began to climb. The current U.S. trend (see graph, p. 25) is depicted by a sharp upward curve during adolescence. The chart line peaks in the twenties and levels off until the fifties, where it starts climbing again, even higher.

[1] Michael Peck, "Youth Suicide," Institute for Studies of Destructive Behaviors and the (Los Angeles) Suicide Prevention Center, 1980.

What explains this upsurge in youth suicide? The fact that some other advanced industrial countries *(see box, p. 34)* share in the upsurge suggests some obvious possibilities, having to do with changes in the structure of society, a more frenzied pace in everyday life, and, especially in America, divorce and family disintegration.

Some psychologists relate America's postwar baby boom to the increase in youth suicide. Children born between 1950 and 1955 passed through their teens and early twenties during the time the suicide rate was rising most quickly. The number of people in that age group was higher than it had ever been. Dr. Peck writes: "It's possible that an overcrowding phenomenon occurred in this generation that resulted in too many young people wanting too many things that are not available, contributing to an increased feeling of anonymity and alienation."

Although theories explaining suicide abound, suicide — especially youthful suicide — remains a mystery. Psychologists and psychiatrists believe that a leading cause of suicide among the young is hopelessness about the future. According to mental health professionals, family relations are crucial in understanding the suicidal person. In recent years, another line of research has been the biochemistry of the brain and its relationship to depression. But since the psychological and physical tend to be interrelated, the question of cause-and-effect remains baffling.

That no one really understands why human beings commit suicide is a disconcerting thought to a society nurtured in the belief that science may admit to the unknown but not the unknowable. It is also a very unsatisfying thought to people who, at least since biblical times, have been sorely troubled by self-inflicted death. And a self-inflicted death by a young person is the most troubling of all. Childhood suicides "fill us with a more than ordinary sense of horror and shame and loss," a novelist has observed.[2]

Characteristics of Suicidal Youngsters

Suicide claims the lives of four times as many boys and young men as it does girls and young women. And the suicide rate among young whites of either sex is consistently higher than among blacks, although there is some evidence that the gap has narrowed a bit. Although fewer teen-age girls than boys commit suicide, they are three times more likely than boys of their age to attempt it. Women are more inclined to ask for help in a crisis, either directly or through suicide attempts — which authorities see as "cries for help" rather than actual attempts to die. This explains why women tend to use less violent and less

[2] Scott Spencer, "Childhood's End," *Harper's*, May 1979.

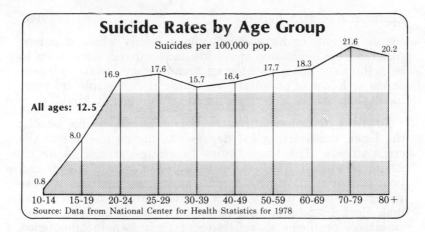

Suicide Rates by Age Group

Suicides per 100,000 pop.

All ages: 12.5

0.8	8.0	16.9	17.6	15.7	16.4	17.7	18.3	21.6	20.2

10-14 15-19 20-24 25-29 30-39 40-49 50-59 60-69 70-79 80+

Source: Data from National Center for Health Statistics for 1978

effective methods, such as pills. Men, on the other hand, are more likely to resort to shooting or hanging, where the chance of survival is small.

Although authorities say they cannot determine that one type of personality is more prone to suicide than another, they have identified certain characteristics that many suicidal young people share. Intense feelings of loneliness, hopelessness and helplessness are universal among suicidal young people. Suicidal adolescents tend to have above-average intelligence and are, like most adolescents, extremely sensitive. Those who are depressed are enormously pessimistic about the future. Dr. Herbert Hendin, who has treated many college students who attempted suicide, reports that "death, depression and unhappiness seem to have been with them since childhood, and have been built into their relationships with their parents."[3]

Typically, suicidal young men have lost a father through death or divorce before age 16. If the father is alive, he is likely to be a business or professional man heavily involved with his work, who never developed a close relationship with his son. Frequently, suicidal sons of these fathers have spent time in schools away from home. Girls who commit suicide often have domineering, self-centered mothers and ineffectual fathers. These girls often turn to boyfriends for support and feel let down when they do not receive the kind of love they are searching for. Mental health experts agree that for both sexes, fathers are central figures.[4]

It has been estimated that two-thirds of the suicidal young people are on poor terms with their families, and that 90 percent feel that their parents do not understand them. Suicidal young people may have experienced child abuse, had an al-

---

[3] Quoted by Margaret O'Hyde and Elizabeth Held Forsyth, *Suicide: The Hidden Epidemic* (1978), p. 68.

[4] See Calvin J. Frederick, "Trends in Mental Health: Self-Destructive Behavior Among Younger Age Groups," National Institute of Mental Health, 1976.

coholic parent, or have come from a family where a parent suffered from depression or suicide had occurred. Some seem to be ambivalent about growing up because they equate independence with loss of parental love. These young people are more likely than others to be devastated by loss of any kind.

Dr. Peck describes four categories of suicidal young people: the loner, those acting out depression, the psychotic and the crisis suicide. The loner begins to emerge at age 14 or 15. Characteristics include loneliness, isolation, lack of friends and poor communication with parents and peers. Families of these young people are usually intact and the parents relatively normal. Peck found that the parents frequently interpret their children's problems as reflective of their own incompetence. They often react defensively by insisting that the child is not really unhappy and has nothing to complain about. The child learns to distrust his or her feelings and ceases to talk to anyone about unhappy thoughts or feelings. These children become high suicide risks as teen-agers.

Another group of suicide risks, those acting out depression, are often impulsive, hostile and disruptive. They are likely to take drugs and alcohol, commit petty crimes like shoplifting, run away from home and even become violent. These young people are also likely to come from broken homes where, according to Peck, chaos, inconsistency and drug and alcohol abuse are common.

The psychotic category of suicides is somewhat smaller than the others, contradicting the myth that all people who kill themselves are insane. Psychotic young people who are suicidal often have delusions and hallucinations and "hear" voices telling them to kill themselves. Most often these young people come from single-parent families or families in which only one parent is psychologically present. Sometimes the parents are psychotic, alcoholic or both.

Youth Suicide Rates
(per 100,000 persons)

Age Group	Total	Males	Females	Whites	Other Races
10-14	0.8	1.2	0.4	0.9	0.5
15-19	8.0	12.8	3.1	8.7	4.5
20-24	16.9	27.4	6.4	17.5	13.8

Source: National Center for Health Statistics, 1980 reporting based on 1978 statistics

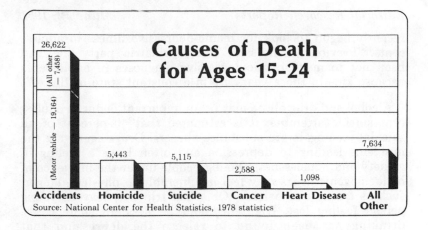

Causes of Death for Ages 15-24

26,622
(All other — 7,458)
(Motor vehicle — 19,164)

Accidents · 5,443 Homicide · 5,115 Suicide · 2,588 Cancer · 1,098 Heart Disease · 7,634 All Other

Source: National Center for Health Statistics, 1978 statistics

Crisis suicide is also a small category, probably representing less than 15 percent of all suicidal young people, according to Peck. Typically these children have no history of emotional problems and come from fairly stable families. However, when faced with sudden traumatic changes such as the loss of a loved one or academic or athletic status at school, these young people may undergo dramatic behavior changes and show classic depressive symptoms.

Social, Psychic and Family Factors

Suicide involves several complex and overlapping factors, none of which acts independently. Most experts believe that a contributing factor is adolescence itself, the most intense developmental phase of all, "bringing with it more changes than are produced in the rest of life put together."[5] According to French child psychologist Didier-Jacques Duche, "adolescence is a 'suicidogenic' period by definition: too many changes taking place too fast."[6] Adults seldom realize teen-agers' vulnerability.

Another factor is depression. At least two-thirds of the people who kill themselves each year in this country suffer from some form of depression, according to Dr. Calvin Frederick, chief of the disaster and emergency mental health section of the National Institute of Mental Health (NIMH). Although not all depressed people attempt or commit suicide, the risk of suicide is 50 percent greater for victims of depression.

Manic-depression, a type of depression that frequently results from biochemical reactions in the brain, has been linked to suicide, particularly when suicides occur in succeeding generations. This suggests a genetic factor — a subject of relatively recent research. According to Dr. Chester Schmidt, a Baltimore psychiatrist who has done suicide research, people have only

[5] André Haim, *Adolescent Suicide* (1970), p. ix.
[6] Quoted in *The Guardian Weekly*, May 25, 1980.

recently begun to look for manic-depressive illness in adolescents. "Previously," he said, "the psychiatric 'party line' had been not to make manic-depressive diagnoses in adolescents because kids in those years are in a constant state of flux."[7]

Alcohol and drug abuse may be an important factor in adolescent suicide attempts; it is estimated that 40 percent of all suicidal teen-agers are substance abusers. Drugs aggravate the problems leading to depression and often leave a feeling of anxiety and hopelessness. Young people under the influence of hallucinogenic drugs may feel invulnerable to physical danger, such as traffic and heights. Or a bad trip may leave a young person feeling lost, frightened and helpless. In some cases, drinking has been found to release the depression that precipitated a suicide attempt. According to NIMH, in suicidal deaths of adults, alcoholism has been a problem in one out of five instances. There is also a high incidence of alcohol abuse among adults who attempt suicide.

Many see the breakdown in the nuclear family — manifested by soaring divorce rates, more children living in single-parent families and child abuse — as leading to emotional isolation, a key factor in youth suicide. Deprivation of love is a common theme in the lives of suicidal children and young people. Young children who are ignored, not touched or made to feel unwanted may eventually respond by taking their own life. According to psychotherapist Jackie Schiff, ignored children develop a craving for stimulation. Because it soon stops mattering to children whether the stimulation is positive or negative, children may seek any kind of stimulation they can get; "it's easier to beat your head against the wall than it is to get someone to hold you," Schiff said.[8]

Overt abuse or severe punishment in childhood is another determinant of suicidal behavior. Writing in the *American Journal of Psychotherapy* on "How Suicidal Behaviors are Learned," Drs. Calvin Frederick and H. L. P. Resnik said: "The child learns to treat himself as others have and to reduce his tension as well as his parents' anger through whippings. As the youngster grows older, self-punishment . . . may precede punishment from others and gain reinforcement, especially if the youngster is in conflict with himself at the time."[9]

Sigmund Freud, the father of psychoanalysis, saw suicide as an act of hostility, a way to kill the image of a person, both loved

[7] Quoted by Jon Reisfeld in "Suicide Ends Four Young Lives," *Baltimore Magazine*, June 1980, p. 80.
[8] Quoted in *Harper's*, May 1979, p. 18.
[9] Calvin J. Frederick and H. L. P. Resnik, "How Suicidal Behaviors are Learned," *American Journal of Psychotherapy*, January 1971, p. 41.

and hated, with whom one identifies. "Kids sometimes wish they could kill their parents, and when they realize they can't they turn their hostility back on themselves," said child psychiatrist Andrew McTaggert.[10] Sometimes children may attempt or commit suicide to manipulate or punish a parent who, they feel, has rejected them.

Prior suicide or suicidal behavior of a family member greatly increases the likelihood that a child in that family will become suicidal. The self-destructive behavior becomes a learning model for a young person searching for ways to deal with problems. A parent's suicide also may induce guilt that later causes the child to feel responsible for the death. These children may feel doomed, or predestined, to kill themselves as their parent did.

Often parents make excessive demands on their children which, when combined with other factors, can literally drive a young person to suicide. Adolescents experience heightened stress in their late teens when they leave home for college. Many college students are overwhelmed by loneliness and feelings of inadequacy, and find that life is not as predictable or safe as they may have thought. In many schools, the pressure to maintain top grades is high and the competition fierce. Often young people who received praise and recognition at home are suddenly faced with their limitations, which can be a painful experience.

Depression: A Leading Cause

IT IS NOT surprising that at a time when 20 percent of all American adults are believed to suffer from some form of depression, young people are struggling with the same paralyzing despair.[11] Dr. Gerald L. Klerman, professor of psychiatry at the Harvard University Medical School, writes that we are living in an age of melancholy, a period when rising expectations clash with limited resources. "A gap that may psychologically predispose individuals to depression," he wrote, "is a gap between expectations and actuality."[12] This would apply to expectations of people's own abilities and their relationships, as well as to expectations of success and accomplishment.

Many psychologists and psychiatrists believe that while social

[10] Quoted by Jane O'Hara in "Young Suicides," *Maclean's,* July 30, 1979, p. 23. McTaggert is supervisor of child psychiatric services at Vancouver (British Columbia) General Hospital.
[11] See "Mental Depression," *E.R.R.,* 1972 Vol. II, pp. 969-988.
[12] Gerald L. Klerman, "The Age of Melancholy?" *Psychology Today,* April 1979, p. 37.

conditions and external events may trigger depression, its source is internal — psychological or biochemical. If causes of depression are difficult to pin down, the effects are more obvious. Depressed young people experience the same symptoms as adults: sleep disturbances, excessive fatigue and lack of energy, loss of or increased appetite, feelings of hopelessness, despair and low esteem, and abrupt and dramatic behavior changes.

Many researchers have observed that delinquent behavior, sexual promiscuity, and drug and alcohol abuse among young people indicate depression. This pattern of behavior is viewed as an attempt to escape from feelings of overwhelming sadness, and to relieve the sense of emptiness and boredom that accompanies depression. This phenomenon, which some psychiatrists call masked depression, is also evident among young children diagnosed as hyperactive and those with school problems or psychosomatic disorders.

In the past there has been uncertainty about the prevalence of depression in young children because the symptoms often do not match those of adults. For example, hopelessness is common among depressed adults and adolescents, but not among children. To feel hopeless a person must be able to think about the future, but young children have difficulty understanding such a concept. Yet about 2 percent of all children are probably depressed, some experts believe. Using criteria recently developed by the American Psychiatric Association, Dr. Jamad Kashani, a child psychiatrist at the University of Missouri Medical school, estimates that there may be over 400,000 depressed children in this country.

Child psychiatrists Leon Cytryn and Donald McKnew of the National Institute of Mental Health have been studying a group of children and grandchildren, aged 4 to 15, of patients admitted to the institute for diagnosis and treatment of depressive psychosis.[13] Besides finding masked depression among these children, they found evidence of what they call acute and chronic depression. The acute type was usually caused by the loss of a relative or someone close. In some cases the loved one had died, but usually he or she — because of a move or personal problems — had simply cut off the care the child had been counting on.

Chronically depressed children, Cytryn and McKnew found, usually had a chronically depressed parent and had been separated several times since infancy from adults they counted on.

[13] See Herbert Yahraes, "Causes, Detection, and Treatment of Childhood Depression," National Institute of Mental Health, 1978.

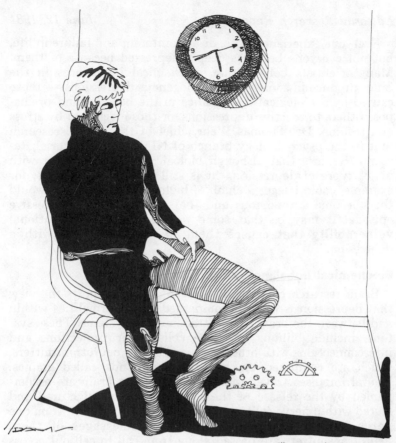

Illustration by Susan Davis

McKnew estimates that about half of the depressed children seen at NMIH have suicidal ideas and see death as a way to escape from unhappy lives.

He reports that some children tie in their suicidal thoughts and actions with their fantasy lives. Young children may want to jump out of a window to fly up to God. Or they may attempt suicide to regain a lost love object, such as one little boy who wanted to jump out of the window to rejoin his dead father in heaven. Because young children often see death as a magical, mystical place and cannot realize death's finality, suicidal gestures among children under 10 are particularly dangerous.

McKnew sees the suicidal gestures of the very young not only as expressions of the wish to stop living, and thus end their psychic pain and loneliness, but also as messages to the world, particularly to the parents. In an interview, McKnew said of the suicidal children he was treating, "I would say that in all cases of desired or attempted suicides mother and father were intended to be spectators. The message is: I'm not very happy. The other message is that it is because of you [the parents]."

31

Everyone experiences loss, disappointment and failure in life, but not everyone becomes deeply depressed because of them. Many scientists believe that biochemical imbalances in the brain produce in some people endogenous depressions — those caused by a biological disturbance in the body — and predispose others to reactive depressions, or those triggered by stress and trauma. Dr. Thomas Wehr, chief of the clinical research unit in the psychobiology branch of NIMH, told Editorial Research Reports that although biologic changes do occur with major types of depression, "it is still possible that stress, for example, could trigger a chain of biological changes that would then become autonomous and [be] expressed as a depressive episode. It may be that some people have a constitutional vulnerability that causes them to react to stress with a depression."

Biochemical Imbalances in the Brain

Brain research conducted in recent years supports the view that depression is often accompanied by abnormalities within and between the brain's neurotransmitting systems. These systems include billions of nerve cells, their projections and interconnections with other nerve cells, and neurotransmitters, which are composed of chemical compounds called amines. Neural impulses traveling in and out of the brain are accompanied by the release of these amines — manufactured and stored within nerve cells — which convey information from one nerve cell to another. The chemical messages of these neurotransmitters are passed along from cell to cell out across the synapse, a small gap between nerve cells. The synapse is the critical spot, where the chemical action is completed or goes awry.[14]

An imbalance of brain amines or an imbalance between the systems they are connected with may impair the transmission of messages across the synapse, thus affecting the entire central nervous system and possibly producing symptoms of depression. Three amines in particular — dopamine, norepinephrine and serotonin — have been identified with symptoms of depression. Abnormalities in dopamine levels have been associated with schizophrenia as well as depression. Norepinephrine is what is released by nerve cells when a person gets "high" from amphetamines; this compound is related to stimulation and mania, a kind of hyperactivity of the emotions. Serotonin has been implicated in sleep disturbances and the presence or absence of pain, as well as personality disturbances.

Researchers have related serotonin deficiencies to people with

---

[14] See "Brain Research," *E.R.R.*, 1978 Vol. II, pp. 661-680.

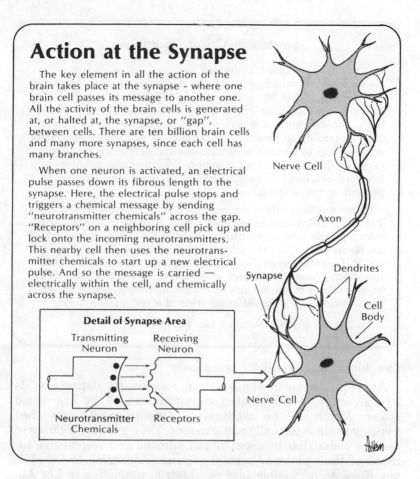

Action at the Synapse

The key element in all the action of the brain takes place at the synapse - where one brain cell passes its message to another one. All the activity of the brain cells is generated at, or halted at, the synapse, or "gap", between cells. There are ten billion brain cells and many more synapses, since each cell has many branches.

When one neuron is activated, an electrical pulse passes down its fibrous length to the synapse. Here, the electrical pulse stops and triggers a chemical message by sending "neurotransmitter chemicals" across the gap. "Receptors" on a neighboring cell pick up and lock onto the incoming neurotransmitters. This nearby cell then uses the neurotransmitter chemicals to start up a new electrical pulse. And so the message is carried — electrically within the cell, and chemically across the synapse.

Nerve Cell

Axon

Synapse

Dendrites

Cell Body

Nerve Cell

Detail of Synapse Area

Transmitting Neuron

Receiving Neuron

Neurotransmitter Chemicals

Receptors

aggressive or impulsive behavior. Specifically, serotonin levels have been found to be low in people who commit violent suicides or make violent suicide attempts. In a recent study conducted by Dr. Marie Asberg of the Karolinska Institute in Stockholm, Sweden, serotonin levels were checked in people admitted to an intensive care unit after attempting suicide. Those with low serotonin levels were ten times more likely to complete a suicide during the following year than were others who had normal or high serotonin levels.

If the roots of depression are biochemical, it is possible that genetic factors may be involved. One area now under study is the genetic "loading" of depression in families. Some studies have shown that children of depressed or manic-depressed parents may be 30 to 50 percent more likely to become depressed as the children of other parents. Although such a finding indicates genetics at work, it is also possible that the children's depression may be caused by the depressed parents' emotional limitations and the resulting home environment.

Suicide in Other Countries

Other industrialized countries are also experiencing an increase in youth suicide and suicide attempts. In West Germany, 1,468 young people 10 to 24 years old killed themselves in 1976, almost twice the number in 1966. In Canada and France, suicide is the second cause of death, after accidents, of 15- to 24-year-olds. According to French authorities, 15- to 19-year-olds make up only 8 to 10 percent of the population in France but account for 17 to 19 percent of all suicides. French youth in their early twenties represent 7 to 10 percent of the population and 22 percent of the suicides.

Japan's suicide rate is comparable to that of the United States. Police in Tokyo estimated that about a third of the Japanese young people who committed suicide in 1977 did so because of problems related to their education. Kichinosuke Tatai, a professor at Tokyo University of Agriculture and an expert in suicide, has said: "Japan's entrance-examination system is one of the biggest causes of suicide among our young people, and this makes the phenomenon here different from the rest of the world."*

*Quoted in *The Wall Street Journal*, Dec. 5, 1978

Low Blood Sugar and Its Symptoms

Another physical abnormality related to depression is hypoglycemia, a diet-related condition caused by low blood sugar. Much of the medical establishment insists that hypoglycemia is virtually non-existent, but a growing number of doctors claim that it is a common ailment and responsible for much of their patients' mental anguish. According to Dr. Harvey Ross, an orthomolecular psychiatrist practicing in Los Angeles,[15] "hypoglycemia has been estimated to affect 10 percent of the United States population."[16] Symptoms of hypoglycemia include fatigue, irritability, confusion, dizziness, anxiety — and depression. Ross reported that Dr. Stephen Gyland, a physician who treated over 600 patients for hypoglycemia, compiled a list of symptoms and their frequency of occurrence. Over 70 percent experienced depression and over 20 percent had suicidal impulses.

Hypoglycemia occurs when the body can no longer regulate the amount of sugar in the blood. The sugar level then drops too far or too fast. The person may experience confusion, hunger (usually for sweets and sometimes for starchy food or alcohol), tremulousness and weakness. Such symptoms are likely to be

[15] The term "orthomolecular psychiatry" was coined by chemist Linus Pauling, a Nobel laureate. The approach is nutritional and involves, in part, giving patients large doses of certain vitamins and minerals.
[16] Harvey M. Ross, "Hypoglycemia," *Journal of Orthomolecular Psychiatry*, 1974, p. 240. The journal is published by the Academy of Orthomolecular Psychiatry at Regina, Saskatchewan, Canada.

temporary and may be relieved by eating. But the more debilitating symptoms of fatigue, irritability, depression and anxiety last longer and cannot be relieved immediately by eating, particulary by eating sugar, which is commonly thought of as an "energy" food.

Known causes of hypoglycemia are tumors or enlargement of parts of the pancreas (the producer of insulin, which is released into the bloodstream where it destroys excess sugar), liver diseases, and adrenal and other endocrine diseases. Many physicians believe that the most common type of hypoglycemia is caused by eating an excessive amount of carbohydrates, particularly the quickly absorbed carbohydrates of sugar and white flour.

According to Ross, co-author of *Hypoglycemia: The Disease Your Doctor Won't Treat* (1980), the physical and psychological symptoms of hypoglycemia are related to lack of nutrients, the probable effect of a high sugar intake on neurotransmitters in the brain, and the effect of the regulatory changes in the body needed to correct its sugar level. When the sugar level drops too low or too quickly, adrenalin is released, which in turn causes the release of stored carbohydrates. In a person with hypoglycemia, adrenalin may be released several times a day. It is the adrenalin that accounts for the nervousness and anxiety that many hypoglycemics experience. Hypoglycemia is treated by eliminating sugar from the diet and making other dietary adjustments.

Evaluation and Intervention

MENTAL HEALTH professionals are rarely the first people to detect a potential suicide. The people in regular contact with a suicidal person — parents, family physician, friends and teachers — are more likely to see a crisis developing. Hence, they need to know what to look for and what to do. Mental health care professionals believe that suicides, especially of young people, can be prevented since most suicidal young people are ambivalent about taking their lives. It is believed that few really want to die; they simply want the pain to stop.

Often suicidal people communicate a subtle or indirect message about their intent to friends, family members or teachers. If nothing else, their behavior may communicate their feelings to those aware of the signs. Verbal clues might include statements like, "I might as well be dead," "you won't have to worry about me much longer," or "you would be better off without me." It is a myth that those who talk about suicide do not go through with it. A young person who talks about wanting to die is likely to attempt suicide.

Another suicide signal is preparation for death, which for a young person might be giving away prized possessions like a record collection or a favorite book. The parents of a suicidal eight-year-old found a will she had written. Another little girl handed her father a rock and asked him to smash her skull. Signals from young children may not always be so clear. Self-destructive behavior for children might include repeatedly running in front of cars, putting staples through their hands or cutting themselves with scissors.

Sudden changes in mood or behavior that last a long time are also suspect. Shy people who become outgoing or adventurous for no apparent reason or friendly people who become withdrawn and apathetic may be depressed and considering suicide. Other clues indicating depression are uncommunicativeness; irritability; fatigue; changes in eating and sleeping habits; reckless or abusive behavior; a marked increase or decrease in sexual activity; loss of interest in school, friends and other activities; preoccupation with death and lessened fear of death. Increased use of drugs or alcohol, although not necessarily evidence of suicidal thoughts, may precede a suicide attempt or signal a deep depression that could become suicidal when the drugs no longer ease the emotional pain they are being used to relieve.

How to Give Psychological First Aid

Of course the most basic preventive measures parents can take is to be attentive, supportive, empathetic and loving toward their children and show them, through example, positive ways to cope with stress. Fostering open communication is also important. Dr. Donald McKnew suggests that parents concerned about their children ask them direct questions such as: Do you feel bad about yourself? Do you ever feel there is no hope in life? Are you lonely? Do you ever want to hurt yourself?

The most important response to suicidal young people is to take them seriously. Often friends or parents dismiss suicidal clues because the person giving them does not seem unhappy or the type to contemplate suicide. Yet depression is not necessarily a precondition for suicide nor is medical science able to determine that one type of personality is more prone to suicide than another. Parents and friends also may dismiss distress signals as adolescent melodrama, overreaction or attempts to get back at them. Experts agree that people who have made suicidal comments or who display evidence of severe depression

Suicide Prevention Centers

There are over 200 suicide prevention centers across the country that are staffed around the clock, seven days a week. The number of calls they receive each year is growing, and several centers are developing programs to accommodate areas in nearby communities. No one knows how many lives are saved through these centers, since many people who call for help may not intend to kill themselves, and untold numbers of suicidal people do not call at all.

Follow-up studies done by the Los Angeles Suicide Prevention Center show that of the callers who were questioned a short time afterward, 87 percent said they had been helped. When questioned a long time after they called, 80 percent said they had been helped, 28 percent said the center had saved their lives, and 34 percent said calling the center might have saved them.

Many suicide prevention centers belong to the American Association of Suicidology (2459 South Ash, Denver, Colo. 80222), a 13-year-old organization of professionals and concerned lay people who believe that public awareness of suicide will help prevent it. Through its programs, publications and activities, the AAS tries to encourage research, education, training and services that can help people recognize and respond to suicidal behavior.

(either directly or by acting out) should be asked if they are contemplating suicide and if they are, what plans — if any — have been made. If plans are detailed, the risk of an actual attempt is greater than if plans are vague.

Rather than implant the idea of suicide, such questions will relieve young people by letting them know that they are taken seriously and give them an opening to talk about their suicidal feelings and impulses. These are terrifying especially to young people, who fear that if they think about killing themselves they might not be able to stop themselves from doing it.

The best help anyone can give most suicidal youngsters is simply to listen and try to understand the feelings behind the words. According to Dr. Peck, "the deterrent [to suicide] is almost always on an interpersonal level — someone saying, in effect, 'Wait, there has to be an alternative. I care about you and want to help you find it.' "[17] People talking with suicidal youngsters are advised not to try to analyze their behavior nor try to shock or challenge them out of the idea (they might accept the challenge). Nor should they argue with the youngsters about whether they should live or die.

It is considered particularly important not to try to convince suicidal young people that suicide is wrong, that they should be

---

[17] Quoted in the *New York Times Magazine*, January 16, 1979.

grateful for what they have since so many others are worse off, or that everything is really all right. If the potential victim believed that, he or she would not be suicidal. Such statements add to their feelings of hopelessness and worthlessness and their belief that no one understands them.

Those dealing with a suicidal young person need to give the impression that they know what they are doing and provide support by letting the person know that everything possible is being done to help. Reassurance should be offered that depressed feelings are temporary and that there is always a chance that problems can be resolved as long as life exists. It should be mentioned that if death is the choice, it is a final one and cannot be reversed. If a young person is acutely distressed, he or she should not be left alone.

People dealing with suicidal youngsters or who are uncertain about their intent should get help. Doctors, members of the clergy or mental health professionals contacted through a community mental health center, suicide prevention center or a telephone crisis "hot line" can give advice about what to do in various situations. Outside help is essential for people who have already attempted a suicide.

Question Over Use of Drug Therapy

A European study conducted by Swiss psychiatrist Walter Poldinger has indicated that suicide rates among young people can be lowered 12 to 15 percent with the use of anti-depressants. According to Dr. Barry Garfinkel, a Canadian authority on youth suicide, the suicide rate is rising among young people "because pediatricians and family doctors don't recognize depression in children and are not treating it with anti-depressant drugs."[18]

Controversy surrounds the use of anti-depressant drugs for children and teen-agers. Some psychiatrists believe that since there is growing evidence that depression is biochemically based, it would be foolish not to use drugs to combat depression's harmful effects. But many doctors believe that such drugs are dangerous — particularly for children — because they could so easily be given to children in whom depression is not the primary problem, or else the wrong drug could be prescribed to a psychotically depressed child with disastrous effects.

According to child psychiatrist Donald McKnew, there does not seem to be a conclusive way to discern the difference between depressions that are biological and psychological. "We don't fool around with lithium [an anti-depressant]," for example, he told Editorial Research Reports, "unless there's a good

[18] Jane O'Hara, "Young Suicides," *Maclean's*, July 30, 1979, p. 22.

Families of Young Suicides

A suicide in the family is a tremendous burden for the survivors. There is still a stigma attached to suicide, particularly that of a teen-ager. Aside from the sense of loss that comes with any death, survivors must deal with the fact that others may hold them responsible for the suicide or the emotional problems associated with it. Survivors also may suffer emotional crises related to the suicide that could cause them to become suicidal themselves.

A recent study conducted in Alberta, Canada,* questioned 90 relatives and friends of young suicides. Most parents felt responsible in some way for their child's death — that either they had caused the suicide or could have prevented it. It is extremely difficult, but important, for survivors to talk openly about their grief and guilt. Mental health experts recommend immediate and continued psychological treatment for the surviving family members.

*Study cited in *Maclean's*, July 30, 1979, p. 23

family history of manic-depression or a major depressive disorder involved." Other doctors believe that among adolescents there is danger of overdosing. Many doctors combine anti-depressant drug treatment with other forms of psychotherapy.

Short-term hospitalization is advised for young people who have attempted suicide, to protect them from harm and contain their anxiety. Suicidal young people also should receive some form of counseling or other psychotherapy even after their release from a hospital. Therapists and counselors try to show young people that they have options; that suicide is not the only way to deal with what they perceive to be an unbearable life.

Dr. Cynthia Pfeffer, a psychiatrist in New York City, believes that educating clinicians about suicidal behavior in young children will improve early evaluation and intervention. She suggests that every child who receives a psychiatric evaluation be assessed for early warning signs of potential suicide.

Dr. Frederick of NIMH believes that guilt should not automatically be assigned to families of young suicides. He agrees with other mental health experts that suicide is everyone's concern. Teachers, clergy, police, parents and young people themselves need to be trained to spot depression, family and school problems, and potentially suicidal behavior. "I think we need to have a massive education program," he said.[19]

It is difficult for most people to think about death, for we fear that which we do not understand. The suicide of a young person

---
[19] Quoted by Jon Reisfeld, *op. cit.*, p. 54.

may be even harder to face — and accept — than death itself. Nonetheless, the growing number of young suicides demands attention and heightened efforts to understand who is at risk and why. Psychiatrist Seymour Perlin wrote, "Coming to terms with suicide will not only help save lives but will offer us an opportunity to enhance our understanding of the human condition, this human dilemma and ourselves."[20]

[20] Calvin J. Frederick and Louise Lague, "Dealing with the Crisis of Suicide," Public Affairs Committee, November 1978, inside cover.

Selected Bibliography

Books

Haim, André, *Adolescent Suicide,* International Universities Press, 1970.
Hyde, Margaret O. and Elizabeth Held Forsyth, *Suicide: The Hidden Epidemic,* Franklin Watts, 1978.
Jacobs, Jerry, *Adolescent Suicide,* Wiley-Interscience, 1971.

Articles

Crumley, Frank E., "Adolescent Suicide Attempts," *Journal of the American Medical Association,* June 1, 1979.
Gardner, Sandra, "Suicidal Behavior," *Senior Scholastic,* June 9, 1981.
Jerome, Jim, "Catching Them Before Suicide," *New York Times Magazine,* Jan. 14, 1979.
O'Hara, Jane, "Young Suicides," *Maclean's,* July 30, 1979.
Pfeffer, Cynthia R., "Suicidal Behavior of Children: A Review with Implications for Research and Practice," *American Journal of Psychiatry,* February 1981.
Reisfeld, Jon, "Suicide Ends Four Young Lives," *Baltimore Magazine,* June 1980.
Spencer, Scott, "Childhood's End," *Harper's,* May 1979.
"Suicide Belt: Rates Up for Affluent Teens," *Time,* Sept. 1, 1980.

Reports and Studies

Editorial Research Reports: "Brain Research," 1978 Vol. II, p. 661; "Mental Depression," 1972 Vol. II, p. 971; "Anatomy of Suicide," 1963 Vol. II, p. 703.
Frederick, Calvin J. and Louise Lague, "Dealing with the Crisis of Suicide," Public Affairs Committee Pamphlet 406A, 1978.
——"Trends in Mental Health: Self-Destructive Behavior Among Younger Age Groups," National Institute of Mental Health, 1976.
Peck, Michael, "Youth Suicide," Institute for Studies of Destructive Behaviors and the (Los Angeles) Suicide Prevention Center, 1980.
Yahraes, Herbert, "Causes, Detection, and Treatment of Childhood Depression," National Institute of Mental Health, 1978.

TEEN-AGE DRINKING

by

Jean Rosenblatt

**May 15
1 9 8 1**

Editor's Note: Five states raised their drinking ages in 1982. Connecticut, New York and Texas raised their legal limits from 18 to 19, Ohio raised its age for beer only from 18 to 19, and Maryland raised its limit from 18 to 21 for wine and beer. That state already had a legal drinking age of 21 for hard liquor.

This summer the National Transportation Safety Board sent letters to governors and legislators in the 35 states where liquor is available to people under 21, recommending they raise their legal limits to 21. Richard S. Schweiker, head of the Department of Health and Human Services, announced Aug. 30, 1982, that his department would launch a program to combat teen-age drinking in the fall.

New laws were enacted this year in 33 states increasing penalties for drunken driving. The most far-reaching of these statutes took effect Sept. 1 in Massachusetts, making it impossible for repeat offenders to avoid penalties. It requires a mandatory 60-day sentence for anyone convicted of drunken driving for a third time. The penalty also includes a fine of $500 to $1,000 and loss of driver's license for five years. Second offenders must spend a week in jail or two weeks in an alcoholism residential treatment center and face a two-year license suspension and a $200 to $1,000 fine. First offenders must pay a fine of at least $100 and have their licenses suspended for 30 days, but no jail sentence is required.

TEEN-AGE DRINKING

M ANY PEOPLE view teen-age drinking as a rite of passage, a natural part of the transition from childhood to adulthood. In fact, teen-agers usually are given their first drink at home and most grow up to be fairly moderate drinkers. But there is evidence that teen-agers start drinking younger, and drink more often and in greater quantities than in the past. And the consequences of their drinking have become more serious. Around 40,000 young people are injured, maimed or killed each year in drunken driving accidents (see p. 47).

"Alcohol abuse is the number one youth drug problem today," according to the National Institute on Alcohol Abuse and Alcoholism (NIAAA).[1] The dimensions of the teen-age drinking problem were underscored by two nationwide surveys conducted for NIAAA by the North Carolina-based Research Triangle Institute. Approximately 15 percent of the 10th- to 12th-graders interviewed in 1978 and 11 percent of the 7th- to 12th-graders interviewed in 1974 were either at the "substantial risk" level or were already problem drinkers.[2]

In the early 1970s many states lowered their legal drinking age from 21 to either 18, 19 or 20, a trend that accelerated after ratification of the 26th Amendment, on June 30, 1971, giving 18-year-olds the right to vote (see p. 50). But now some states are having second thoughts. In the past five years 14 states have banned the sale of alcohol to 18-year-olds, and in some states, to 19- and 20-year-olds, as well (see box, p. 52). No state has lowered its legal drinking age since Alabama did so in July 1975.[3] "Our studies have shown that ease of availability is related to heavier drinking," said J. Valley Rachal of the Research Triangle Institute. "Those states that allow 18-year-olds to purchase alcohol have heavier drinking. And that's reflected in a growing tendency to move the laws to a higher age."

The North Carolina researchers found little change between

---

[1] National Institute on Alcohol Abuse and Alcoholism, "Alcohol Topics in Brief: Alcohol and Youth," November 1980, p. 3.
[2] Results of the surveys reported in "Fourth Special Report to the U.S. Congress on Alcohol and Health," Department of Health and Human Services, January 1981, p. xxii.
[3] Oklahoma in 1976 passed a law allowing 18-year-olds to purchase beer with 3.2 percent alcohol content.

1974 and 1978 in the percentage of adolescent alcohol users, the frequency of teen-age drinking and the quantity of alcohol involved. But they emphasized that the proportion of young people who have ever used alcohol has stabilized at a fairly high level and that a substantial number drink fairly regularly. Over 80 percent of the high school students surveyed in 1978 said they had had a drink in the year prior to the survey, while over 20 perent reported drinking once a week or more. Over 8 percent reported drinking three or four days a week and nearly 2 percent reported drinking every day. Approximately 31 percent said they had been drunk at least six times in the year prior to the survey — often enough for the researchers to label them "alcohol misusers."[4]

A 1979 survey conducted for the National Institute on Drug Abuse[5] found that alcohol is the drug students try most often and are most likely to continue to use. More than twice as many teen-agers and young adults regularly drink alcoholic beverages as regularly use other drugs *(see box, p. 48)*. Over 75 percent of the 18- to 25-year-olds surveyed and over 37 percent of the 12- to 17-year-olds said they had had a drink in the past month. In contrast, 35.4 percent of the young adults and 16.7 percent of the 12- to 17-year-olds said they had recently used marijuana.

Various Influences on Teen Drinking Habits

Most young people give the same reasons for drinking as adults: to celebrate an occasion, to feel good, to go along with the crowd, to release tension or to cope with problems. Teen-agers often begin using alcohol out of curiosity or to appear grown-up. "When teen-agers drink," wrote Dr. Margaret Bacon, "the best explanation of their behavior is that they are adopting the pattern set by the majority of adults."[6]

Some 56 percent of the students responding to the NIAAA's 1978 survey said they drank "to have a good time." Since alcohol reduces inhibitions (by shutting down certain brain impulses), it is not surprising that awkward, insecure teen-agers, worried about their appearance and their effect on the opposite sex, might seek out its relaxing effects. Along with the social awkwardness of adolescence comes the desire to break away from the family and the equally strong desire to fit in with peers. Teen-agers are much more likely to drink with their friends than with family or other adults. In fact, 22 percent of the respondents to the 1978 survey said that they frequently drank while driving around or sitting in a car at night.

---

[4] J. V. Rachal, et al., "A National Study of Adolescent Drinking Behavior," National Institute on Alcohol Abuse and Alcoholism, 1980.
[5] National Institute on Drug Abuse, "National Survey on Drug Abuse: Main Findings 1979," Department of Health and Human Services, 1980.
[6] Margaret Bacon and Mary Brush Jones, *Teen-age Drinking* (1968), p. 47.

The legal status of alcohol apparently makes its use acceptable to many students who do not use other drugs. According to a spokesman for the Washington, D.C., Area Council on Alcoholism and Drug Abuse, many teen-agers do not consider wine or beer — the most popular alcoholic drinks among young people — as harmful as hard liquor. Alcohol also is cheaper and easier to obtain than such drugs as marijuana and cocaine and gives a satisfactory "high." Also, the penalties are far less serious for under-age drinking than for using illegal drugs.

Many parents seem unconcerned about their children's drinking habits. "Adult America's fondness for booze makes us reluctant to deal with the problem...," *Human Behavior* magazine suggested in its August 1978 issue. "Many parents, in fact, are relieved to find their offspring are 'only drinking' and not messing with pot or hard drugs." Morris E. Chafetz, the former director of the National Institute on Alcohol Abuse and Alcoholism, made a similar observation in 1972: "Non-alcoholic drugs are somehow foreign and frightening, because their use, except as medicine, is not yet accepted as part of the mainstream of American culture. Alcohol, on the other hand, is so common a drug that we tend to ignore it — and its victims."[7]

Extent and Consequences of Problem Drinking

There are an estimated 12 million to 14 million problem drinkers in this country, including 3 million teen-agers. Alcohol misuse among young people is most often associated with episodic, heavy drinking than with alcoholism. Teen-age problem drinkers usually do not suffer from the physical disabilities, such as liver damage, associated with alcoholism. "Those concerned with the biomedical aspects of alcohol use do not really know how to define alcoholism in terms of teen-agers," J. Valley Rachal said in a recent interview. "And the prevalence of alcoholism in teen-agers is, at best as can be determined, very low."

The young problem drinker, as distinguished from typical adolescent drinkers, uses alcohol more often, in larger amounts and usually for the purpose of getting drunk. He or she is also more likely to display aggressive or destructive behavior and to drink alone. Excessive drinking is generally related to emotional problems — inability to meet goals set by parents, rejection or abuse by parents, lack of love or quarreling between parents — which make the child feel insecure or unwanted. For some teen-agers, alcohol may psychologically replace an unavailable or

[7] National Institute on Alcohol Abuse and Alcoholism, "Alcohol & Alcoholism: Problems, Programs and Progress," 1972, p. iii. Chafetz is now president of the Health Education Foundation in Washington, D.C.

available or rejecting parent. "These children symbolically ingest that individual when they drink, and it becomes as difficult to separate them from alcohol as it is to break a close human bond," said Stephanie Brown, associate director of the Alcohol Clinic at Stanford University Medical Center.[8]

The importance of the family in the transmission of drinking habits is demonstrated by the high correlation between offspring and parent with regard to types of beverages used, drinking frequency and amounts consumed. There is evidence that the children of alcoholics are high risks for becoming alcoholics themselves. Although there is little evidence to support genetic inheritance of alcoholism, the fact that children of alcoholic parents are more prone to the disease suggests the significance of the family environment.

Although teen-age problem drinkers do not usually suffer from the physical symptoms that occur in adult alcoholics, including physical dependence on alcohol, many have their lives totally disrupted by drinking. "The increase in teen intoxication is of great concern to all of us...," psychologist Patricia O'Gorman, former director of the NIAAA's division of prevention, told Editorial Research Reports. "It's not so much the drinking itself, although we're concerned about that — it's the consequences of the drinking."

Problem drinking among adolescents has been linked with precocious sexual behavior, poor school performance, frequent absences from school, higher dropout rates, incidences of vandalism and disorderly conduct, problems within the family, and use of other drugs. In fact, many young people use alcoholic beverages in combination with other drugs, especially marijuana. Such use produces a synergistic effect — an effect greater than the total of what the drugs could produce individually. Thousands of deaths — accidental or suidical — occur each year among persons who take barbiturates or tranquilizers while intoxicated.

No nationwide statistics have been collected on the connection between teen-age drinking and suicide. Some experts believe that up to 40 percent of the teen-agers who kill themselves each year may have been abusing alcohol or other drugs.[9] Patricia O'Gorman agrees that alcohol is a factor in a significant number of teen-age and college-age deaths. "It may be hard to know whether [an alcohol-related death] was a suicide or an

---

[8] Quoted in "Growing Teen-age Drinking Problem," *U.S.A. Today,* February 1980.
[9] See David Martindale, "Why the Young, the Rich, the Educated, are Choosing Suicide," *Glamour,* October 1979, p. 142. According to the National Center for Health Statistics, about 5,000 people under age 25 committed suicide in 1979, the last year for which complete figures are available.

Alcohol Consumption of Teen-agers and Young Adults

	Youth (12-17)	Young Adults (18-25)
Recency:		
Drank alcoholic beverages in past month	37.2%	75.9%
Drank in past, not in past month	33.3	19.4
Within past six months	10.3	7.2
Six months to a year ago	6.1	3.5
More than one year ago	9.8	6.5
Not sure	7.1	2.2
Always a non-drinker	29.7	4.7
Days used in past month:		
Current drinkers	37.2	75.9
Number of days:		
One to four	26.0	36.7
Five to nine	4.8	14.9
Ten to nineteen	3.1	12.1
Twenty or more	1.0	10.2
Not sure	2.6	2.1
Greatest alcohol consumption on any one day in past month:		
Current drinkers	37.2	75.9
Number of drinks:		
One or two	19.1	23.1
Three or four	6.7	18.2
Five to ten	8.7	24.8
Eleven or more	2.1	9.6
Not sure	.9	*

Some categories do not add to 100% because of rounding.
*Less than .5%.

Source: National Institute on Drug Abuse, "National Survey on Drug Abuse, 1979."

accident. . . ," she said. "Certain kids will chug-a-lug a fifth of vodka and asphyxiate themselves — basically put their brain to sleep — and they die. . . . These kids are not trying to kill themselves. Death is an unintended consequence of drinking."

Impact of Alcohol on Traffic Accident Rate

Traffic accidents are the major cause of violent deaths in the United States. Between 35 and 64 percent of the drivers involved in fatal automobile accidents had been drinking prior to the accident. The ratio of alcohol-related fatalities is even greater among teen-agers. Between 45 and 60 percent of all fatal

Drug Use Among Teen-agers and Young Adults

	Youth (12-17)		Young Adults (18-25)	
	Ever Used	Current User	Ever Used	Current User
Alcohol	70.3%	37.2%	95.3%	75.9%
Cigarettes	54.1	12.1	82.8	42.6
Marijuana	30.9	16.7	68.2	35.4
Inhalants	9.8	2.0	16.5	1.2
Hallucinogens	7.1	2.2	25.1	4.4
Cocaine	5.4	1.4	27.5	9.3
Heroin	.5	*	3.5	*
Stimulants	3.4	1.2	18.2	3.5
Sedatives	3.2	1.1	17.0	2.8
Tranquilizers	4.1	.6	15.8	2.1
Analgesics	3.2	.6	11.8	1.0

*Less than .5 percent.

Source: National Institute on Drug Abuse, "National Survey on Drug Abuse, 1979."

crashes involving a young driver are alcohol related.[10] "The drunk-driving problem in this country has reached epidemic proportions," said John Moulden, a research psychologist with the National Highway Traffic Safety Administration. "It's a national outrage that even when thousands of people are being killed each year by drunk drivers, our society continues to accept drinking and driving as a normal part of daily life."[11]

The FBI reports that in 1979, the latest year for which statistics are available, 190,847 persons under age 21 were arrested for driving under the influence of alcohol; in 1967, only 17,807 persons in that age group were arrested for the same offense. Nearly a quarter of the students responding to the 1978 NIAAA survey admitted that they often drove after having had a good bit to drink. In 1978, according to the National Safety Council in Chicago, Ill., drivers under age 20 were involved in 11,500 crashes with at least one fatality. There were about 5.6 million reported traffic accidents that year caused by drivers between the ages of 15 and 20.[12]

In most states a person is considered legally drunk when his or her blood registers a .10 percent alcohol content. According to the Distilled Spirits Council of the United States, a 150-pound man would have to drink four 1-ounce shots of 100-proof liquor

[10] "Fourth Special Report to Congress on Alcohol and Health," p. xxvi. Nearly 26,000 Americans die each year in drunken driving accidents, the leading cause of highway deaths in the United States.
[11] Quoted in The Washington Post, March 22, 1981.
[12] National Safety Council, "Accident Facts, 1979," 1980.

48

or four 12-ounce cans of beer in an hour to achieve this limit. Maryland and Mississippi allow a blood-alcohol content of .15 percent, which for a 150-pound man amounts to six shots of 100-proof liquor or six 12-ounce cans of beer in an hour.[13]

Many teen-agers believe that beer is safer to drink than hard liquor or mixed drinks. In fact, the alcoholic content of one can of beer is nearly equal to that of a 1½-ounce shot of 80-proof liquor. Also, the amount of alcohol consumed and the frequency with which it is consumed affect adults and teen-agers differently. It takes much less alcohol to impair a teen-ager's ability to drive, for example, than an adult's. It has been found that teen-agers involved in fatal car crashes often have lower alcohol concentrations in their blood than do adults involved in similar accidents. A study by the National Public Service Research Institute found that over half the teen-agers involved in alcohol-related accidents had blood-alcohol levels of only .02 percent, a level produced by about one drink and a concentration considerably below the level legally recognized as drunk.[14]

Special Problems Faced by Adolescent Girls

Teen-age boys still drink more and in greater quantities than girls. But there is evidence that adolescent girls may be experiencing more drinking problems than in the past. According to NIAAA figures, about 60 percent of female high school students drank in the 1970s, compared to 25 percent in the previous decade. Marian Sandmaier, author of *The Invisible Alcoholics: Women and Alcohol Abuse in America* (1980), reports that since World War II drinking among young women has increased more rapidly than it has among young men, that teen-age girls are starting to drink younger and more heavily, and are more likely to drink hard liquor than in the past.

"Although relatively few teen-age girls could be termed clinically alcoholic," Sandmaier wrote, "thousands are drinking to the point where it is interfering with their schoolwork, damaging relationships with family and friends, contributing to unwanted sexual encounters and sometimes pregnancies, causing accidents and arrests, and generally undermining their emotional and physical health." Yet parents and juvenile authorities seem more reluctant to recognize drinking problems in girls than in boys, possibly because there is a greater expectation for girls to be "good." Among the reasons parents give for denying a daughter's drinking problem, Tom Alibrandi wrote in *The Young Alcoholics*, are "[f]ear that a daughter might be stealing, sleeping around, or suffering from a sullied reputation."

---

[13] Revisions now being considered in Maryland would lower the legal blood-alcohol level to .10 percent.
[14] See "Teen-age Drinking and Driving," *Better Homes and Gardens*, July 1979.

Teen-age girls drink for the same reasons boys do. Girls who abuse alcohol usually have extremely low self-esteem, and their drinking often contributes to problems that reinforce their feelings of worthlessness. Teen-age girls may be especially susceptible to male peer pressure, according to one researcher. In a series of studies of high school and college drinking patterns in Walla Walla County, Wash., between 1972 and 1974, Lee H. Bowker found that girls were influenced by the drinking and drug use patterns of boyfriends much more than boys were influenced by girl friends' drug use. Among college students, young women were likely to be "turned on" for the first time to alcohol, marijuana and other drugs by young men, while the men were more likely to be given drugs and alcohol by other men. And while 70 percent of the men bought their own alcohol and drugs, only 11 percent of the women did.

Two-thirds of the fraternity men responding to a college survey conducted by Bowker admitted using alcohol and other drugs to make their dates "more sexually willing or responsive." According to Marian Sandmaier "such findings suggest that many young women may begin drinking in relatively powerless situations, in which their own judgment about when and how much to drink may be subordinated to their boyfriends' control over both the liquor supply and the dating situation."

Legal Battle To Control Abuse

RATIFICATION of the 26th Amendment in 1971 giving 18-year-olds the right to vote[15] sparked movements in many states to grant young people full majority rights, including the right to drink. The rationale was that persons eligible to vote and to serve in the armed forces were old enough to handle alcoholic beverages. Between 1971 and 1975, 19 states lowered the legal drinking age to 18.[16] In addition, seven states voted to allow 19-year-olds to buy and drink at least some alcoholic beverages.[17] Delaware in 1972 lowered its legal drinking age to 20.

Many people viewed the trend toward lowering the legal drinking age as a realistic and logical way to help young people

[15] See "Politics and Youth," *E.R.R.*, 1970 Vol. I, pp. 259-277.
[16] Conn., Fla., Ga., Hawaii, Iowa, Maine, Md., Mass., Mich., Minn., Mont., N.H., N.J., R.I., Tenn., Texas, Vt., W.Va. and Wis. Louisiana lowered its legal drinking age to 18 in 1948, New York in 1934.
[17] Ala., Alaska, Ariz., Idaho, Ill., Neb. and Wyo.

adapt to a predominantly drinking society. The Cooperative Commission on the Study of Alcoholism, in a 1967 report, said that the age limit of 21 "is largely unenforceable and in addition creates a basically hypocritical situation reminiscent of the Prohibition era."[18] But law enforcement officials in states where the drinking age was lowered to 18 reported an increase in liquor law violations involving young teen-agers. "They lowered the age by three years, so now we have 15-year-olds slipping around getting drinks purchased by 18-year-olds they associate with," said one official in the Nashville, Tenn., police department. "I'm afraid we are so worried about getting their votes we forgot about their physical and mental well-being."[19]

The strongest opposition to legalizing liquor sales to teen-agers came from highway safety authorities who feared that the combination of inexperienced drinkers and inexperienced drivers would add to the carnage on the nation's highways — a concern that seemed to be borne out by the statistics. A 1974 study noted that after Michigan lowered its minimum legal drinking age to 18 on Jan. 1, 1972, alcohol-related accident rates among 18- to 20-year-olds increased by 18 percent.[20] In Massachusetts, where the drinking age was lowered to 18 in 1973, researchers reported a 40 percent increase in fatal accidents involving young people ages 18 to 20.

Researchers with a Washington, D.C., group called Medicine in the Public Interest reviewed several studies showing an increase in youths involved in traffic accidents following a lowering of the minimum-age law. They concluded that "the actual extent of the increase and its significance . . . are not clear."[21] A few of the studies they reviewed suggested that the change in law had more effect on the perception of alcohol involvement or the police reporting procedures than it did on the fatal crash rate of young drivers.

Current Move to Raise Legal Drinking Age

Of the 27 states that lowered their legal drinking ages, 14 have raised them again *(see box, p. 52)*. Over a dozen states — including some that already have raised their drinking age once — are considering further or first-time raises. Except for Michigan and Illinois, none of the states that increased their minimum drinking age went back to 21; most raised the minimum to 19. Including Michigan and Illinois, 19 states now ban liquor

---

[18] Thomas F. A. Plaut, "Alcohol Problems: A Report to the Nation by the Cooperative Commission on the Study of Alcoholism" 1967, p. 149.
[19] Quoted in *U.S. News & World Report*, Nov. 13, 1972.
[20] R. L. Douglass, "The Effects of Lower Legal Drinking Ages on Youth Crash Involvement," University of Michigan Highway Safety Research Institute, 1974.
[21] Medicine in the Public Interest, "The Effects of Alcohol-Beverage-Control Laws," 1971, p. 69.

States That Have Raised The Drinking Age

State	Former Minimum	Current Minimum	Effective Date	State	Former Minimum	Current Minimum	Effective Date
Fla.	18	19	10/80	Minn.	18	19	9/76
Ga.	18	19	9/80	Mont.	18	19	1/79
Ill.	19	21	1/80	Neb.	19	20	8/80
Iowa	18	19	7/78	N.H.	18	20	5/79
Maine	18	20	10/77	N.J.	18	19	1/80
Mass.	18	20	4/79	R.I.	18	19*	7/80
Mich.	18	21	12/78	Tenn.	18	19	6/79

*Effective July 1, 1981, drinking age will be 20.

Source: Distilled Spirits Council of the United States Inc.

sales to persons under age 21; the other states are Arkansas, California, Colorado, Indiana, Kansas, Kentucky, Missouri, Nevada, New Mexico, North Dakota, Ohio, Oklahoma, Oregon, Pennsylvania, South Dakota, Utah and Washington.[22] South Carolina, Maryland, Mississippi and Virginia forbid those under age 21 from buying hard liquor but permit them to purchase wine and/or beer.

Virginia Gov. John Dalton signed a measure last February forbidding anyone under age 19 from buying beer at liquor package stores. Other types of alcoholic beverages remain out of bounds for all 18- to 20-year-olds in the state. In neighboring Maryland, legislators considered bills that would have raised the legal drinking age for beer and wine. The state Senate approved a measure that would have raised the minimum from 18 to 19. But the Maryland House of Delegates in April voted down a bill to raise the statutory minimum to 21.

Public support for raising minimum drinking ages is strong. A 1979 Gallup Poll taken in 24 states allowing 18-year-olds to buy and drink alcoholic beverages found that 56 percent of the adults queried favored raising the drinking age to 20 or 21; 39 percent thought the legal drinking age should remain at 18; 4 percent had no opinion. A popular argument in favor of raising the drinking age to 19, 20 or 21 is that such a move would prevent high school seniors from buying alcohol for their younger schoolmates. *The Milwaukee Journal* reported a few years ago that "of almost 4,000 alcohol-related incidents in schools in the fall of 1976, 18-year-old pupils supplied the beverage in half of the cases."

J. Valley Rachal of the Research Triangle Institute maintains that "teen-agers in states with lower drinking ages are, in fact, drinking more" than young people in states with higher statu-

[22] Some states permit 18-year-olds to purchase beer with not over 3.2 percent alcohol content.

tory minimums. But other experts believe the relationship between minimum drinking ages and teen-age alcohol consumption is not that clear. Mary McFadden, an attorney with the child welfare unit of the Massachusetts Department of Public Welfare, and Henry Wechsler, director of research at The Medical Foundation in Boston, conducted three surveys of teen-age drinking in five Massachusetts communities (in 1965, 1970 and 1974) and a 1977 survey of college students at 34 New England colleges and universities. Their findings indicated an increase in teen-age drinking after the drinking age was lowered in Massachusetts in 1973.

But according to McFadden and Wechsler, the increase began long before the age was lowered, "and the major part of the increase" actually occurred before the law was changed. "The change in the law may be more reflective of an already occurring change in drinking behavior, rather than a subsequent change," they concluded.[23] Their college survey, on the other hand, indicated that the students perceived drinking age laws to have deterred their drinking somewhat.

Debate Over Laws' Influence on Teen-agers

Some experts argue that raising minimum drinking ages will encourage 18- to 20-year-olds to drink in unmonitored situations such as parties or on the highways rather than in the more controlled atmosphere of a college pub or a tavern. Others say that raising the drinking age punishes 18-year-olds without dealing directly with the drunken driving problem, which led investigators and the public to reconsider the lowered ages in the first place. These critics believe that the evidence showing a correlation between lowered drinking ages and higher rates of alcohol-related accidents is not conclusive and have cited a Massachusetts study that showed an increase in arrests for drunken driving in Massachusetts after the minimum age was raised from 18 to 20 in 1979.

Another popular view is that legal age requirements do not prevent teen-agers from getting alcohol, particularly since many teen-agers get their liquor at home. "It's pretty well established that laws in and of themselves do not change social customs," said Dr. Gerardo Gonzalez of the University of Florida.[24] Others agree that changing laws will not change the causes of teen-age drinking, which are symptomatic of a larger societal problem with alcohol consumption. According to Dr. Gail Milgram of the Center for Alcohol Studies at Rutgers University, treating teen-age drinking as the central issue "takes the focus off all the 35-year-olds that have alcohol-related highway accidents." Focus-

[23] Mary McFadden and Henry Wechsler, "Minimum Drinking Age Laws and Teen-age Drinking," *Psychiatric Opinion*, March 1979, p. 23.
[24] Quoted in *The New York Times*, May 18, 1980.

State Minimum Drinking Ages

	Distilled Spirits	Wine	Beer		Distilled Spirits	Wine	Beer
Ala.	19	19	19	Mont.	19	19	19
Alaska	19	19	19	Neb.	20	20	20
Ariz.	19	19	19	Nev.	21	21	21
Ark.	21	21	21	N.H.	20	20	20
Calif.	21	21	21	N.J.	19	19	19
Colo.	21	21	21[1]	N.M.	21	21	21
Conn.	18	18	18	N.Y.	18	18	18
Del.	20	20	20	N.C.	21	21[2]	18
D.C.	21	21[2]	18	N.D.	21	21	21
Fla.	19	19	19	Ohio	21	21	21[1]
Ga.	19	19	19	Okla.	21	21	21[4]
Hawaii	18	18	18	Ore.	21	21	21
Idaho	19	19	19	Pa.	21	21	21
Ill.	21	21	21	R.I.*	19	19	19
Ind.	21	21	21	S.C.	21	18	18
Iowa	19	19	19	S.D.	21	21	21[1]
Kan.	21	21	21[1]	Tenn.	19	19	19
Ky.	21	21	21	Texas	18	18	18
La.	18	18	18	Utah	21	21	21
Maine	20	20	20	Vt.	18	18	18
Md.	21	21[2]	18	Va.	21	21	18
Mass.	20	20	20	Wash.	21	21	21
Mich.	21	21	21	W.Va.	18	18	18
Minn.	19	19	19	Wisconsin	18	18	18
Miss.	21	21[2]	21[3]	Wyo.	19	19	19
Mo.	21	21	21				

[1] Age 18 for 3.2 percent beer.
[2] Age 18 for light wine.
[3] Age 18 for beer having not over 4 percent alcohol by weight.
[4] Age 18 for 3.2 beer, off-premise consumption.
* Effective July 1, 1981, 20 years old.

Source: Distilled Spirits Council of the United States, March 1981.

ing on the narrower issue of teen-age drinking, she said, "does something to ease our conscience ... and yet there's no positive framework established for helping adolescents deal with the society in which we live, which happens to be a drinking society." Echoing the belief that adults possibly are shifting responsibility from themselves to their children, syndicated columnist Ellen Goodman wrote: "Rather than trying to educate our children in ... morality and values, we are embarked on a major attempt to scare them straight."[25]

[25] Column in *The Washington Post*, March 31, 1981. Goodman was writing about sex education.

No one really believes that raising minimum drinking ages will solve the problem of teen-age drinking. But Medicine in the Public Interest has made the cautious claim that there are indications of a "high level" of compliance to age limits among under-age young people. The group said that even though a minimum-age law frequently may be violated, it may help prevent drinking among some young teen-agers. McFadden and Wechsler recommended that states considering raising their legal drinking age consider whether the benefits of higher ages "offset the ambiguity and incongruity of treating youth as adults for some acts but not for others."[26]

Treatment and Prevention

MOST EXPERTS agree that children should be educated about alcohol use at an early age, before attitudes, values and behaviors become fixed. Many also believe that the schools are the most logical setting for alcohol education programs. According to current research, 6- and 7-year-olds have already developed attitudes about drinking alcoholic beverages. Some programs now include curricula for grades as low as kindergarten.

In most states, alcohol education is mandated by law. According to a recent survey done by the National Clearinghouse for Alcohol Information, 93 percent of high schools offer some type of alcohol curriculum. Community agencies, public health departments, community alcohol centers, alcoholism councils and mental health centers also sponsor alcohol education programs either on their own or cooperatively with a school system.[27]

Educators have tried several different approaches to alcohol education over the years, including factual lectures about what alcohol will do to the body and mind if you drink enough of it, and scare tactics featuring gory films of fatal traffic accidents and the diseased organs of alcoholics. But teen-agers frequently are unconcerned with the future and turned off by preaching about the evils of alcohol or attempts to make them feel guilty about their behavior. Many eduators believe that the most effective education and prevention methods help young people

---

[26] McFadden and Wechsler, *op. cit.*, p. 23.
[27] See National Institute on Alcohol Abuse and Alcoholism, "Guide to Alcohol Programs for Youth," 1980.

develop decision-making and refusal skills; that is, how to say no. They favor programs that focus on clarifying values, minimizing the risks of drinking, solving problems, recognizing one's feelings and coping with anxiety, and developing self-esteem.

Educators also believe it is important for programs to present alternatives to drinking and to encourage young people to understand the role that drinking plays in American society. In *The Young Alcoholics*, Tom Alibrandi wrote that it is important for alcohol education programs to dispel myths about alcoholism in terms young people can understand. "When presenting information about alcohol," he added, "it is equally important to point out what constitutes social drinking, thus setting a standard of accepted alcohol use."

One problem with alcohol education programs is inadequate teacher training. Dr. Gail Milgram of Rutgers University's Center for Alcohol Studies told Editorial Research Reports that some states that have mandated alcohol education have chosen not to have it as part of their teacher training package. "So we've got teachers out there who are concerned and caring who sometimes have not had any more information than the students. They think they should be doing something, and if they do, it is sometimes based on their own prejudice."

Family Involvement in Treatment Programs

Although most teen-agers with alcohol-related problems are not alcoholics, many need some form of treatment. In general, prevention and early intervention are the most effective ways to reduce alcohol problems of young people, since the earlier a child can be identified as a problem drinker the more likely the negative consequences of his or her drinking can be prevented.

Because many teen-agers start drinking at home and drink partly to emulate adults, many believe that the solution to teen-age problem drinking lies within the family. But Dr. Milgram thinks it is a mistake to put all the burden on the family. "I don't think we can say parents must handle this because they can't, they haven't, and they won't," she said. Often the parents of teen-age problem drinkers have alcohol problems themselves or are slow to get their children help because they do not recognize — or they deny — that a problem exists.

Ideally, alcohol education and prevention is a cooperative venture, with parents, schools and the community participating. Such comprehensive programs can educate adults as well as teen-agers about alcohol and its abuse, and also give adults the opportunity to re-examine their own drinking attitudes and behavior. "Any kind of therapy or treatment for the young alcoholic is minimally effective unless parents are also involved," Tom Alibrandi wrote in *The Young Alcoholics*. "The kid-fix-it-shop approach — mom and dad drop off their alcoholic-abusing young one for a carburetor tuning or a tire patch and pick the youngster up all fixed — is a myth. The entire family needs a healing experience."

Alibrandi described the work of the Alcoholism Council of Orange County, Calif., which includes the parents of teen-age alcohol abusers sent there by the courts. The program holds separate sessions for parents and their children. Counselors there have found that joint sessions work best only in residential centers, where the young people are not using alcohol or drugs. While a child is still misusing alcohol, confrontations with parents often confuse the issue and sometimes encourage the child to drink more. One of the program's goals is to diffuse the resentment between parents and child by helping the parents detach themselves from their child's behavior. This also helps the children by forcing them to face the consequences of their own behavior.

Counselors ask the parents to back up their talk with action by setting limits on their children's behavior around the house. The parents are then asked to deal with the behavior appropriately if their child does not stay within the limits. Parents are advised not to protect their children from the system and to let authorities handle misbehavior outside the home. Counselors also advise parents to require their children to pay for court fines, lawyer fees and repairs for damaged property or to treat such costs as a loan if their teen-ager cannot pay. Finally, counselors suggest that parents require their alcohol-abusing teen-agers to get jobs and not cover for them when they arrive late, do not show up or cannot function.

New Strategies for Helping Teen-age Girls

In *The Invisible Alcoholics* Marian Sandmaier wrote: "Even if a young woman's drinking problem is finally recognized, help is often hard to find. Most teen-age alcohol and drug programs are geared to the needs of young men, and girls regularly drop out of such programs or are refused admittance in the first place." One center that does deal specifically with alcohol and drug problems of teen-age girls is New Hope Manor, set up by four nurses in 1972 in Manchester, Conn. New Hope now houses 11 residents and has a capacity for 15. Its program tries to help young women abusing drugs and alcohol to build stronger self-concepts and deal with daily life without resorting to drugs or alcohol.

The young women living at New Hope Manor explore such problems as guilt about sexual relationships, difficulties in making friends, conflicts about their femininity and low self-esteem. "Every girl who has walked into New Hope Manor has felt rotten to the core about herself," said Joanne Stowell, the program's director. "How else can they feel, when everything associated with their alcohol and drug abuse is contrary to the feminine role they're expected to adopt? Most of them have been arrested, expelled from school, shunned by girl friends, rejected by boyfriends. And, yes, most of them have been sexually abused." Stowell believes girls have a harder time than boys coping with their alcohol and drug problems. "There's no doubt that drinking and drug abuse cause [boys] serious problems," she said, "but at the same time they can prove their manhood — by sexual prowess, by flaunting authority. But girls feel they have failed totally."[28]

Research on women's drinking problems has been limited, but preliminary findings suggest some guidelines for preventing alcohol abuse among teen-age girls. Experts suggest that girls get help in dealing with specific situations such as dating and alcohol. They should learn about the risks associated with women's drinking problems, such as the danger of combining alcohol with prescription drugs and recent findings on the effects of alcohol on the unborn. Teen-age girls also need to learn how to handle alcohol abuse by males, since alcohol is a factor in up to 50 percent of rape and family violence cases.[29]

Assertiveness Training and Meditation

Since the early 1970s, significant numbers of young people have been showing up at Alcoholics Anonymous and other alcoholic treatment and rehabilitation centers. AA now has a number of youth-oriented clubs around the country. Very few alcoholic treatment facilities are designed specifically for teenagers. Some authorities worry that young problem drinkers could feel overwhelmed in a clinical program for adult alcoholics. "If you have a 14-year-old with alcohol problems, there's no place for them really to go," said psychologist Patricia O'Gorman. "There are some specific services for teens but they are model programs. You are not going to find them as part of the health service delivery system, and we need to have that."

One model program is the Adolescent Alcohol Abuse Treatment Center in lower Manhattan in New York City, which offers short-term crisis intervention services, as well as alcoholic treatment and rehabilitation to inner-city young people. Although individual, family and group counseling is available, the program mainly uses "milieu therapy," or the creation of a total

---

[28] Quoted by Sandmaier in *The Invisible Alcoholics*, p. 169.
[29] See "Violence in the Family," *E.R.R.*, 1979 Vol. I, pp. 305-324.

environment to promote positive interactions, self-expression, responsibility and independence. Individualized treatment. plans and services like family planning and vocational training are also part of the program.

Assertiveness training and meditation have been found to be useful tools in some treatment programs. Assertiveness training can help young people learn to express anger and other feelings appropriately and directly, thereby diffusing some of the frustration that often accompanies problem drinking. Young people with severe drinking problems are usually anxious and have low self-esteem. Some studies have shown that regular meditation can help reduce tension, improve self-esteem and help remove the craving for drugs. In one survey 40 percent of the subjects who meditated regularly for more than 2 years said they stopped drinking alcohol within the first 6 months.

Tom Alibrandi tried using meditation as a therapeutic tool with prison inmates, 90 percent of whom abused alcohol and other drugs. He found that meditating prisoners generally showed less anxiety than inmates who did not meditate as well as decreased boredom, resentment against authority, depression and drug abuse. Their health and ability to get along with others also seemed to improve.[30] Alibrandi acknowledged that most young alcohol abusers, unless they have stopped drinking, will stop meditating before they experience the benefits of meditation. He is now doing more research on the use of meditation with drug and alcohol abusers.

The attention given the alarming number of traffic accidents and fatalities involving teen-age alcohol abusers seems to have aroused a panic about teen-age drinking comparable to the drug scare of the late 1960s and early 1970s. Yet Drs. Morris E. Chafetz and Howard T. Blane urge policymakers not to overreact to the subject of alcohol and youth. They believe that drinking behavior is learned and strongly subject to parental and peer influence, and that therefore prevention through education has enormous potential.[31] In the meantime, more research is being done on the extent of young people's drinking and alcohol-related problems to determine how teen-age alcohol misuse and abuse can be reduced.

---

[30] See Tom Alibrandi, *The Meditation Handbook* (1976).
[31] Morris E. Chafetz and Howard T. Blane, "High School Drinking Practices and Problems," *Psychiatric Opinion*, March 1979, p. 17.

Selected Bibliography

Books

Alibrandi, Tom, *The Young Alcoholics,* CompCare Publications, 1978.
Blane, H. T. and M. E. Chafetz, eds., *Youth, Alcohol, and Social Policy,* Plenum Press, 1979.
Haskins, Jim, *Teen-age Alcoholism,* Hawthorne Books, 1976.
Mayer, John E. and William J. Filstead, eds., *Adolescence and Alcohol,* Ballinger, 1980.
Sandmaier, Marian, *The Invisible Alcoholics: Women and Alcohol Abuse in America,* McGraw-Hill, 1980.

Articles

Chafetz, Morris E. and Howard T. Blane, "High School Drinking Practices and Problems," *Psychiatric Opinion,* March 1979.
"Closing the Tap: Trend against Legal Drinking by 18-year-olds," *Time,* Feb. 26, 1979.
"Going Back to the Booze," *Time,* Nov. 5, 1979.
McFadden, Mary and Henry Wechsler, "Minimum Drinking Age Laws and Teen-age Drinking," *Psychiatric Opinion,* March 1979.
"Pro and Con: Raise the Legal Age for Drinking?" *U.S. News & World Report,* April 16, 1979.
"Teen-age Drinking and Driving," *Better Homes and Gardens,* July 1979.
"The Latest Teen Drug," *Newsweek,* Jan. 8, 1979.
Trippett, Frank, "The Young: Adult Penchants — and Problems," *Time,* April 6, 1981.
"Young People and Alcohol," *Alcohol Health and Research World,* summer 1975.

Reports and Studies

Editorial Research Reports: "Resurgence of Alcoholism," 1973 Vol. II, p. 987.
Fishburne, Patricia M., et al., "National Survey on Drug Abuse: Main Findings, 1979," National Institute on Drug Abuse, 1980.
Josephson, Eric, et al., "An Assessment of Statistics on Alcohol-Related Problems," Distilled Spirits Council of the United States, Inc., May 5, 1980.
Medicine in the Public Interest, Inc., "The Effects of Alcoholic-Beverage-Control Laws," 1979.
National Institute on Alcohol Abuse and Alcoholism: "Fourth Special Report to the U.S. Congress on Alcohol and Health," January 1981 (preprint copy); "Guide to Alcohol Programs for Youth," 1980.
Rachal, J. Valley, et al., "A National Study of Adolescent Drinking Behavior, Attitudes, and Correlates," Research Triangle Institute, April 1975.

Cover illustrated by Staff Artist Robert Redding

Marijuana Update

by

Marc Leepson

Feb. 12
1982

Editor's Note: Retail sales of U.S.-grown marijuana rose to about $8.5 billion in 1981. California's marijuana crop last year was worth some $1.5 billion. According to the National Institute on Drug Abuse, the percentage of high-school seniors who have tried marijuana dropped from 60.3 percent in 1980 to 59.5 percent in 1981. The percentage of seniors who used marijuana in the previous year also decreased, from 48.8 to 46.1 percent, as did the percentage of seniors who used the drug in the previous 30 days, from 33.7 to 31.6 percent, and the percentage of daily marijuana users, from 9.1 to 7.0 percent.

MARIJUANA UPDATE

I N NOVEMBER 1974 Dr. Robert L. DuPont, director of the White House Special Action Office for Drug Abuse Prevention, delivered the keynote speech at the annual convention of the National Organization for the Reform of Marijuana Laws (NORML). Dr. DuPont, a psychiatrist and one of the nation's top drug experts, told the gathering that marijuana possession should not be a crime because criminal penalties did little to prevent abuse of the drug. Dr. DuPont continued to speak out for the decriminalization of marijuana after he became head of the National Institute on Drug Abuse (NIDA) in 1975.[1]

But now Dr. DuPont has changed his position. "If you are for decriminalization, you are, in the public mind, for pot," he said recently. "That process has forced me to retreat on my earlier position on decriminalization...."[2] Dr. DuPont says he still does not want marijuana smokers to go to jail. But because of what he believes is new evidence linking marijuana to health problems, Dr. DuPont favors keeping the drug illegal and enforcing the laws against its production, sale and possession.

DuPont's change in thinking symbolizes a recent swing in the public perception of marijuana, a drug that 55 million Americans have tried and 23 million use on a regular basis.[3] At the time Dr. DuPont was speaking out in favor of lowering penalties for marijuana possession there was a strong national marijuana reform movement led by NORML. From 1973 to 1978, 11 states passed laws decriminalizing marijuana (see p. 78). It was a time when marijuana was widely perceived as a harmless social drug — the drug of choice for young Americans, as alcohol was for their elders. During the 1976 presidential campaign candidate Jimmy Carter came out in favor of decriminalization. Carter's adviser on drug policy, Dr. Peter Bourne, was progressive in his views on marijuana, and worked closely with NORML officials.

---

[1] The National Institute on Drug Abuse is a federal agency that conducts research on the prevention, control and treatment of narcotic addiction and drug abuse. Dr. DuPont served as NIDA director from 1975-78.

[2] Quoted by Patrick Anderson in *High in America: The True Story of NORML and the Politics of Marijuana* (1981), p. 312. Dr. DuPont heads a private drug and alcohol abuse organization, the Institute for Behavior and Health, in Bethesda, Md.

[3] Statistics from NIDA's biennial National Household Survey on Drug Abuse conducted by George Washington University.

The shift in the pendulum on the marijuana issue started about the time Dr. Bourne was forced to resign from the Carter White House in July 1978 after he admitted writing an illegal drug prescription for an aide and newspaper reports alleged that he had used cocaine at a NORML party in 1977. Dr. Bourne's successor, Lee Dogoloff, shifted the White House's emphasis on marijuana. President Carter stopped talking about decriminalization, and Dogoloff began meeting with a new constituency, leaders of parents' groups that had begun forming across the country to fight teen-age drug abuse *(see p. 70)*. Since 1978 not one state has decriminalized the drug. NORML's founder and national director Keith Stroup was twice arrested for possession in Canada. When Stroup was forced to resign under fire in 1978 the marijuana reform movement was in disarray.

Today, the conservative Reagan administration has stepped up the government's anti-marijuana campaign, which is aimed primarily at parents' groups and adolescents. NIDA Director Dr. William Pollin last year termed marijuana "a major public health menace for young people," and said the drug has "potentially very grave consequences for their personal future and the nation's future." [4] Peter Bensinger, who resigned as head of the U.S. Drug Enforcement Administration (DEA) last July, characterized marijuana as "the single biggest drug problem we've got in the United States, without question." [5]

Possible Links to Physical Problems

Parental and governmental anti-marijuana fervor has been fueled in recent years by medical studies linking the drug with a number of physical problems. The most recent evidence suggesting marijuana is harmful was released late last year by the Addiction Research Foundation in Canada. According to the foundation's president, John D. Macdonald, the report concluded that marijuana "is a powerful drug with a broad range of risks to health." [6] Other recent studies have linked marijuana use to the impairment of intellectual performance, the lessening of the body's immune reponse (the natural defense against illness), the impairment of some aspects of reproduction and other health problems.

---

[4] Testifying Oct. 21, 1981, before the Subcommittee on Alcoholism and Drug Abuse of the Senate Labor and Human Resources Committee.

[5] Appearing on "The MacNeil-Lehrer Report," PBS-TV, July 2, 1981. DEA was established in 1973 by President Nixon as an independent unit within the Justice Department. It is the primary federal law enforcement agency responsible for combatting drug abuse. Under a reorganization plan announced in January 1982, DEA began working with the FBI for the first time. Previously the FBI became involved only in drug cases linked to organized crime. Bensinger, who was appointed DEA head by President Ford in January 1976, resigned in July 1981 in protest over Reagan administration budget cuts. Francis M. Mullen Jr., an executive assistant director of the FBI, has served as acting DEA administrator since Bensinger's resignation, and is expected to be nominated to head the agency.

[6] The report was a summation of current thinking on marijuana's health effects based on a meeting of marijuana researchers from 10 nations held in Toronto from March 30 to April 3, 1981. Macdonald's remarks quoted from the foundation's booklet "Cannabis, Health and the Law," October 1981.

Is Pot Stronger Today?

One of the arguments anti-marijuana groups use is that marijuana today is 10 times stronger than the marijuana sold a decade ago. This significantly stronger marijuana, the argument goes, presents a much greater danger to users, especially young persons. One reason for the increased strength of marijuana is that American growers, primarily in California, have increased the content of their product's active ingredient, THC (delta-9-tetrahydrocannabinal). The strongest California marijuana contains as much as 6 percent THC, while ordinary marijuana has as little as 0.5 percent THC.

The higher-potency marijuana has resulted from the cross-cultivation of Mexican, Colombian, Jamaican and American varieties with Asian marijuana. This strong hybrid is then cultivated as *sinsemilla,* a seedless variety formed by culling out male plants from marijuana patches. Sinsemilla plants grow as high as 20 feet tall. Each plant produces about a pound of marijuana.

Kevin Zeese, executive director of the National Association for the Reform of Marijuana Laws, disputes the claim that pot today is 10 times stronger than the marijuana sold a decade ago. That claim is "a great exaggeration," Zeese said in an interview. "Sinsemilla only makes up about 15-20 percent of the marijuana in the United States. The vast majority consumed in the United States is still the lower-quality Colombian, Jamaican and other South American varieties — not the American seedless."

Marijuana's defenders point out that none of the new medical studies has come up with conclusive evidence linking marijuana use to health problems. "There are no new studies" that prove marijuana is harmful, Kevin Zeese, NORML's executive director, told Editorial Research Reports. "What they really are are rehashments of old studies ... I think it's basically a continuation of 'reefer madness' exaggeration." [7] Dr. Norman Zinberg, a top drug expert who is a professor of psychiatry at Harvard Medical School and a member of NORML's advisory board, said in an interview that marijuana can damage the lungs and adversely affect those with heart conditions. "Aside from that," Dr. Zinberg said, "the findings continue to be equivocal. There's enough evidence to follow up, but there is nothing definitive."

There are those in the medical community who think that today's overriding concern about the health effects of marijuana is misplaced. "The reason that marijuana is harmful isn't to do with its medical effects, whatever they might be," said Dr. Anne

[7] "Reefer madness" refers to the U.S. government's shrill anti-marijuana campaign that began in the 1920s. The campaign featured the planting of sensationalistic newspaper accounts of a marijuana "epidemic." At the height of the campaign in 1936, Hollywood released a fictionalized movie done in the style of a government documentary titled "Reefer Madness." The not-so-subtle message in the film was that marijuana leads to madness, murder, rape and pillage. Several years ago NORML bought a copy of the movie, and began showing it to audiences around the country.

Geller, director of the Smithers Alcoholism Treatment and Training Center at New York's Roosevelt Hospital. "It has to do with the fact that kids smoking pot on a constant basis . . . are dropping out of school and are unable to think and do whatever work they have to do. It's having a terrific effect on their occupational potential. The medical effect compared to that is negligible." Dr. Geller said that even if marijuana were shown conclusively to cause detrimental health effects, that fact would not influence many persons to stop abusing the drug. "I've spoken to [alcoholic] patients in liver failure . . . and said, 'Look, this is what alcohol does.' They go right out and start drinking again. . . . I think the reasons they do go beyond medical reasons."

Research Findings Largely Inconclusive

The evidence connecting marijuana to most health problems is inconclusive. There are hints that marijuana use may lead to physical problems, but no firm evidence has been uncovered. On the other hand, even those in favor of marijuana agree that the drug is not entirely harmless, that it has indisputable physiological and psychological consequences. For one thing, smoking marijuana increases the heart beat by as much as 50 percent. Doctors agree that this increase probably is insignificant for healthy individuals, but advise those with cardiac problems or heart disease to avoid smoking marijuana.

Heavy marijuana smoking — like heavy tobacco smoking — is detrimental to the lungs and respiratory system. Marijuana smoke narrows the lung's air passages and causes an inflammation of the sensitive lining of the lungs. Burning marijuana emits more than 150 chemicals, including benzopyrene, a known carcinogen. This is not to say that all heavy marijuana smokers will get lung cancer. But doctors agree that those who smoke marijuana heavily, like those who smoke cigarettes, run a high risk of developing lung problems, including chronic bronchitis and cancer. "The only studies that seem somewhat definitive have to do with lung damage," said Dr. Zinberg. "The evidence is that marijuana causes just as much lung damage as tobacco."

Some marijuana studies have found that the drug may contribute to a decline in sperm concentration and total sperm count. But as with most other areas of marijuana research, the studies are inconclusive and sometimes contradict one another. Other studies have shown lower testosterone (male sex hormone) levels in pot smokers. One study indicated that marijuana may be responsible for menstrual problems in women, as well. Some animal studies suggest a possible relationship between fetal defects and marijuana smoking, but no definitive studies have confirmed this. Drug researchers nevertheless agree that pregnant women and nursing mothers should avoid marijuana and all other drugs.

Opinion is divided as to whether marijuana adversely affects the body's natural defenses against infection and disease. In a study completed in 1974, Dr. Gabriel G. Nahas of Columbia University — a specialist in marijuana research and a longtime critic of the drug — reported that the formation of white blood cells (which are important in fighting off disease) was impaired by as much as 40 percent in subjects who smoked pot. Subsequent research has failed to bear out these findings.

Some of the effects of marijuana on the brain are well documented. Smoking the drug produces a "high," a pleasurable sensation of mild euphoria, a loosening of inhibitions, an intensity of emotions and heightening of the senses. Colors often become more vivid, there is an increased feeling of awareness of the self, and time and space seem to expand.

Marijuana also causes physical changes. Those under its influence often are less physically coordinated than usual. Some act more slowly than usual and have short-term memory lapses. Some users claim that the drug enhances their mental and physical abilities. But laboratory tests indicate that marijuana intoxication interferes with the skills needed to drive an automobile safely. Even marijuana reformers advise those under its influence not to drive.

Heavy marijuana use does not necessarily lead to impairment of mental functions. That was the conclusion of a 1981 study conducted by Dr. Jeffrey Schaeffer of the Department of Psychiatry and Behavioral Sciences at the University of California School of Medicine in Los Angeles. Dr. Schaeffer's study examined a group of people who had smoked 2-4 ounces of marijuana a day over a long period of time as part of a religious commitment. The subjects' ages ranged from 25-36; all were born, raised and educated in the United States. "All subjects actively engaged in daily work, largely agricultural and business, and led active and spiritual lives," Dr. Schaeffer reported. Psychological tests indicated no impairment of mental functioning of any member of the group, and IQ scores were in the "superior to very superior" range.[8]

Schaeffer's study did not prove that heavy marijuana smoking does not harm mental functioning. It merely provided some evidence along those lines. In that respect it resembled the estimated 10,000 experiments on marijuana and health under-

---

[8] Writing in *Science*, July 24, 1981, pp. 465-466. In the subjects' religion, which was not identified, marijuana "symbolized the sacrament of communion." One religious movement that uses marijuana as a sacrament is Rastafarianism, a Jamaican movement founded by Marcus Garvey which believes in the divinity of the late Emperor Haile Selassie of Ethiopia.

taken in the last decade whose results were inconclusive. According to Patrick Anderson, author of a 1981 book on the politics of marijuana, "there is ... a case to be made that the anti-marijuana forces have tried, perhaps with the noblest of intentions, to use very tentative, inconclusive scientific data as a new, more sophisticated version of the reefer-madness campaign of the 1930s. Then the anti-marijuana crusaders warned that marijuana would turn its users into violent criminals. Now the opponents of marijuana say, 'It may make you feel good, but it is actually giving you cancer and/or damaging your brain and/or making you impotent and/or crippling your unborn children.' " [9]

Pot's Potential Therapeutic Benefits

As the debate over marijuana's harmful effects continues, there is growing evidence that the drug has potential medical benefits. Medical practitioners in the ancient civilizations of China, Persia, Greece, Rome and elsewhere used marijuana (or cannibas, or hemp, as the drug also is known) to treat muscle spasms, general pain, digestive problems and other maladies. The Egyptians used marijuana to treat eye problems. During the Middle Ages Europeans used the drug to ameliorate the effects of burns and infections.

Cannabis was not used in modern Western medicine until 1839 when Dr. William B. O'Shaughnessy, an Irish physician who worked in India, published a 49-page article called "On the Preparation of Indian Hemp or Gunjah" in a Bengali medical journal. O'Shaughnessy's work consisted of an extensive review of the literature on the use of marijuana in Indian medicine. The physician also conducted animal and human experiments with patients suffering from seizures, rheumatism, tetanus and rabies. "His most clear-cut findings were that cannabis relieved pain and acted as a muscle relaxant and an anti-convulsant," wrote Dr. Solomon H. Synder of Johns Hopkins University. [10]

Dr. O'Shaughnessy's work stimulated interest in marijuana in Europe. Doctors on the Continent began testing the drug on a wide range of medical conditions, including menstrual cramps, asthma, insomnia and migraine headaches. The first American test was conducted by the Ohio Medical Society in 1860. Soon American physicians began treating and prescribing different marijuana preparations for many ailments. Before Congress outlawed the drug in 1937, many pharmaceutical firms, including Eli Lilly, Parke-Davis and Squibb, sold marijuana extracts and tinctures as health aids.

---

[9] Anderson, *op. cit.*, pp. 316-317.
[10] Solomon H. Snyder, *Uses of Marijuana* (1971), p. 8.

Marijuana Update

Recent medical studies have shown that marijuana may be helpful in treating or alleviating glaucoma, arthritis, asthma and spinal cord injuries. Marijuana is also effective in relieving two unwanted side effects of chemotherapy in cancer patients — nausea and vomiting.[11] The U.S. Food and Drug Administration (FDA) began allowing cancer patients to ingest THC capsules (pills containing delta-9-tetrahydrocannabinal, the active ingredient in marijuana) in September 1980. The capsules must be ordered by cancer specialists through National Cancer Institute-registered hospital pharmacies, and only patients who cannot use any other anti-nausea drugs are permitted to use the THC capsules.

In October 1976 Robert Randall of Washington, D.C., became the first glaucoma patient to receive marijuana legally when the FDA agreed to provide him with government-grown marijuana after medical tests determined that Randall's condition responded favorably to the drug. Then, in 1978, New Mexico became the first state to authorize legal access to marijuana for glaucoma and cancer patients after a cancer victim, Lynn Pierson, led a lobbying campaign in the state legislature. Today, a total of 32 states[12] have enacted similar laws, according to the Alliance of Cannabis Therapeutics, a Washington, D.C., group working to help legalize marijuana for therapeutic purposes.

Issue of Adolescent Use

THE UNITED STATES has the highest level of marijuana use among young people of any developed country in the world. According to NIDA statistics, more than seven million young persons between the ages of 12 and 17 — 31 percent of that age group — report having tried marijuana more than once. Among that group, 50 percent said they had used marijuana five days or more in the previous month. Among high school seniors, over 60 percent have tried marijuana *(see box, p. 71)*. Thirty-one percent of the seniors say they tried pot for the first time before entering high school, usually in the 7th, 8th or 9th grades.

Reports of marijuana use in elementary schools are no longer uncommon. "Several years ago, high school students were experimenting," a Connecticut high school official said in 1980.

---

[11] See "New Cancer Treatments," *E.R.R.*, 1982 Vol. I, pp. 65-84.
[12] Alabama, Arizona, Arkansas, California, Colorado, Connecticut, Florida, Georgia, Illinois, Iowa, Louisiana, Maine, Michigan, Minnesota, Montana, Nevada, New Hampshire, New Jersey, New Mexico, New York, North Carolina, Ohio, Oklahoma, Oregon, Rhode Island, South Carolina, Tennessee, Texas, Vermont, Virginia, Washington and West Virginia.

"Now we are finding that in most cases people coming into high school may have started using it in the fourth, fifth or sixth grade, and got into a heavy dependence by junior high school." [13]

Although it appears that marijuana use among young persons may be declining slightly, the extent of drug use remains a significant problem. This is because young persons are particularly vulnerable to the physiological and psychological side effects of all drugs, marijuana included. "A very real danger in marijuana use is its possible interference with growing up," a NIDA publication warns. "As research shows, the effects of marijuana can interfere with learning by impairing thinking, reading comprehension and verbal and arithmetic skills. Scientists also believe that the drug may interfere with the development of adequate social skills and may encourage a kind of psychological escapism." [14]

Even NORML, the marijuana reform lobbying group, warns against the use of the drug by adolescents. "NORML is opposed to the use of marijuana by kids," said executive director Kevin Zeese. "We say that all adolescents should not use any drugs, including marijuana, including caffeine, including liquor." That comment was echoed by a NORML advisory board member, Dr. Norman Zinberg of Harvard Medical School. When asked what he would say to a 17-year-old in good health who asked whether or not to smoke marijuana, Dr. Zinberg replied: "I would ask him to wait a year or two.... I don't think kids should use anything. I don't want them to drink. I don't want them to smoke. I don't want them to use grass."

Nationwide Growth of Parents' Groups

One reaction to the widespread use of marijuana among teenagers has been the rapid growth of parents' groups concerned about the effects of marijuana on their children. Hundreds of such groups have been formed in the last five years to influence children to stay away from drugs. Among the most active parents' groups are DeKalb County (Ga.) Families in Action, Parents Resource Institute for Drug Education (PRIDE) in Atlanta and the Naples (Fla.) Informed Parents Group. Representatives of parents' groups have lobbied Congress to set up a national drug information center for adolescents and to give financial support to groups set up to stop teen-agers from using drugs. Thus far those lobbying campaigns have been unsuccessful.

[13] David Moxhay, dean of students at Greenwich High School in Connecticut, quoted in *The New York Times Magazine*, Feb. 2, 1980, p. 38.
[14] National Institute on Drug Abuse, "For Parents Only: What You Need to Know about Marijuana," 1981, p. 5.

Marijuana Use Among
High School Seniors

	1975	1976	1977	1978	1979	1980
Have ever used marijuana	47.3%	52.8%	56.4%	59.2%	60.4%	60.3%
Used marijuana in the previous— 12 months	40.0	44.5	47.6	50.2	50.8	48.8
Used marijuana in the previous 30 days	27.1	32.2	35.4	37.1	36.5	33.7
Used marijuana daily	6.0	8.2	9.1	10.7	10.3	9.1

Source: National Institute on Drug Abuse

Parents' groups have been successful in convincing countless local and state governments to set up ordinances and laws banning the sale of cigarette papers, pipes and other paraphernalia used in smoking marijuana.[15] Parents' groups also have gotten radio and television stations to broadcast public affairs announcements that discourage young persons from using marijuana. Some groups work closely with school officials and use school facilities to set up programs to warn children of marijuana's ill effects. Nearly all parents' groups sponsor meetings where children and parents discuss the issue of marijuana use.

Before there were parents' groups there were private drug-treatment centers that worked with parents and teen-agers. The largest drug abuse treatment program in the country is run by New York's Phoenix House Foundation. Its drug-abuse prevention classes are attended by more than 5,000 students a month in the New York City Metropolitan area. These classes are conducted in public, private, parochial and preparatory schools. Phoenix House has a special evening program for parents that teaches them the facts about teen-age drug abuse. The group's message for parents is: "Don't be afraid of saying 'no' to drugs. Take a firm stance. Set the rules: 'Any use is abuse.' You have to be the primary person in your kid's life. Get back into the driver's seat."

New Problem: Parents Who Use Drugs

Drug counselors have recently begun to notice a new variable in the child-parent marijuana equation: parents who use the drug themselves. NORML officials claim that more parents in

[15] The Drug Enforcement Administration has drawn up a model law that 25 state legislatures have passed to outlaw shops that sell drug paraphernalia. Those states are: Arkansas, Connecticut, Delaware, Florida, Georgia, Idaho, Indiana, Kansas, Louisiana, Maine, Maryland, Massachusetts, Montana, Nebraska, Nevada, New Hampshire, New Jersey, New Mexico, New York, North Carolina, Oklahoma, Texas, Vermont, Virginia and Washington. A number of other states have passed laws with similar restrictions.

Drug Use Among Teen-agers and Young Adults

	Youth (12-17)		Young Adults (18-25)	
	Ever Used	Current User	Ever Used	Current User
Alcohol	70.3%	37.2%	95.3%	75.9%
Cigarettes	54.1	12.1	82.8	42.6
Marijuana	30.9	16.7	68.2	35.4
Inhalants	9.8	2.0	16.5	1.2
Hallucinogens	7.1	2.2	25.1	4.4
Cocaine	5.4	1.4	27.5	9.3
Heroin	.5	*	3.5	*
Stimulants	3.4	1.2	18.2	3.5
Sedatives	3.2	1.1	17.0	2.8
Tranquilizers	4.1	.6	15.8	2.1
Analgesics	3.2	.6	11.8	1.0

*Less than .5 percent.

Source: National Institute on Drug Abuse, "National Survey on Drug Abuse, 1979."

the United States smoke marijuana than adolescents. Parents who use marijuana must wrestle with some difficult questions, including whether or not they should smoke in the presence of their children and whether or not they should discourage their children from using marijuana. "It's a very individual matter," said Harvard University psychiatrist Dr. Lester Grinspoon. "I think that the parent who would smoke with an 11-year-old is irresponsible, like any parent who has a drink with an 11-year-old. That's insane because it says 'I believe it is okay for you to drink at your age.' But I know of one instance where a woman smoked dope with her teen-aged kids and she thought it enhanced her relationship with them for her to stop hiding it. I wouldn't be surprised if other people whose kids are 17 or 18 felt the same." [16]

It appears that most parents who smoke marijuana refrain from smoking in front of their children. A 33-year-old father told Editorial Research Reports that he and his wife do not smoke marijuana in front of their six-year-old son. "We smoke in private so that he won't be confronted with the issue until he's able to deal with it in a somewhat mature way," the father said. "When it becomes an issue in his school, we will try to be honest with him about our feelings about marijuana. I think we will tell him it's okay to smoke once a person's body is mature and their physical growth wouldn't be harmed by it. If he asked me whether we smoke, I would be honest and say 'yes.' I would also tell him that it's something that would have to stay between the three of us because it's illegal."

[16] Quoted by *Boston Globe* reporter Judy Foreman in *The Baltimore Sun*, Sept. 27, 1981.

A 41-year-old father told Editorial Research Reports that he is more concerned about alcohol abuse than marijuana abuse with his 15-year-old son.[17] "I'd rather that he smoked than drank," said the father, a regular marijuana user. "But of course I'm not going to tell him that. I sense that booze is coming back as sort of the drug of choice among teen-agers, and I worry mainly because he just got his driver's license. What I really lecture him on is moderation." The father said he would not smoke marijuana in the presence of his son "until he is an adult." The father said he would admit to smoking the drug if his son asked, "but I wouldn't tell him the frequency with which I use it. I would say that I have done it, and that in my own experience I prefer to have it as something I do at home, not while driving, for example. I'd stress moderation here, too, and also warn him that he could get busted unless he's careful."

A 35-year-old mother said she has not smoked marijuana openly at home, nor would she ever consider doing so. If her 14-year-old daughter asked if she smoked marijuana, the mother said she probably would say, "I have used it occasionally." But her advice for her daughter would be: "I'm not telling you never to use it or to try it. I'm saying you're too young now and you should wait.... If you do things like smoke marijuana, drink, smoke cigarettes and so on by the time you're 16, you're going to be pretty bored by the time you're 36."

Combating Pot Use Among Teen-agers

Some parents take a harder line on the question of adolescent drug use than others. Actress Jane Fonda, for example, said recently that if her children — a 13-year-old girl and a 9-year-old boy — ignore her warnings not to use drugs and alcohol, she will "take them right down to the hospital, to the floor where all the burnt-out kids are ... the adolescents with their brains fried. And I will take them through the ward and show them the consequences."

The National Institute on Drug Abuse recommends other, not-so-drastic measures. The institute's advice for parents who think their child has tried marijuana or is smoking regularly is to "remain calm." Emotional and angry outbursts, NIDA says, are counterproductive. They "only interfere with the dialogue that is now essential." [18] The agency suggests that if parents cannot deal with the issue without becoming emotionally overwrought, they should try to get a friend whose advice their child respects to join the family for a discussion of the issue.

NIDA also suggests that parents should not be alarmed if

[17] See "Teen-Age Drinking," *E.R.R.*, 1981 Vol. I, pp. 349-368.
[18] "For Parents Only," *op. cit.*, p. 19.

their children come forward and admit they smoke marijuana. On the contrary, when a child is open about such a sensitive subject, it is a sign that the parent-child relationship is working well. The agency advises parents to try to find out why their child smokes marijuana. The most common reasons are because "everyone else is doing it," and because being high on marijuana feels good. The best way to help a child stop using marijuana is for the parent to help the child deal with peer pressure, rather than to stress the reasons why marijuana may be harmful. One way a parent can work against peer pressure is to meet with other parents and discuss marijuana use among their children.

The institute points out that there is no stigma attached to parents whose children smoke marijuana. "Even children of loving parents who have set a good example and taught moderation can become caught up in drug use," the agency says. As for concrete steps parents can take, NIDA suggests setting up curfews, limits on spending money and the use of the family car to make it harder for teen-agers to gain access to drugs. Children and parents also should take part in events as a family. The most important thing, the agency says, "is not the activity, but that you are taking a personal interest and that your child is developing a focus on things other than drugs." As a last resort, NIDA recommends that parents of heavy drug users "consider seeking help from a doctor or other health professional even if you have to do this without the youngster's consent."

Some teen-agers find professional help in one of a number of private groups around the country formed to break the marijuana habit. Among the largest is the Marijuana Intensive in San Francisco, founded in 1980 by psychologist Joe Reilly. Marijuana Intensive uses methods based on those employed by alcoholic treatment groups such as Alcoholics Anonymous. The treatment aims for total abstinence and offers a four-to-nine week group therapy program for $125.

New York City's Potsmokers Anonymous was begun in 1978, and offers a nine-week course taught to groups of not more than eight persons. According to Perry Izenzon, the group's director, nearly all of those who complete the course wind up kicking the marijuana habit. Potsmokers Anonymous also aims for total abstinence. "We think that people ought to give themselves a period of time to compare," Izenzon said. "They know what smoking marijuana is like. We want to give them enough of the space between their drug taking to see what life is like without pot smoking. We think a year is a fair amount of time." Izenzon said that very few who go through the program continue to smoke marijuana. "Virtually everyone says that [their drug-free year] is the best and most productive year of their lives," she said.

Marijuana and the Law

PRO- AND ANTI-MARIJUANA groups agree that children and adolescents should not use the drug. But there is a wide difference of opinion on the best way to keep marijuana away from minors. Government health officials, parents' groups and others want to continue the current policy of prohibiting the production, sale and use of marijuana. "We need to discourage the use of marijuana," said former DEA Administrator Peter Bensinger. "That means there needs to be enforcement of the laws that we have, and an international effort to reduce availability, and an educational program to provide users, parents, teachers and communities with accurate facts, a realistic description of what risks you run." [19]

Marijuana reform advocates contend that the best way to keep the drug away from adolescents is to lift criminal penalties against marijuana and to regulate its production and sale. "It is the policy of prohibition that has led to the use of marijuana by adolescents," said NORML's Kevin Zeese. "The government has no control over the sale of marijuana to adolescents.... Today it's a lot easier for a kid to buy marijuana than it is to buy alcohol because he can't go out and buy alcohol. That's why marijuana is used more by kids than alcohol — because it's easier for them to get."

Even if marijuana were legalized and regulated, a certain amount would be consumed by adolescents. But marijuana reformers say that legalized marijuana would at least be pure cannabis and not laced with chemicals. "Many times kids get the worst quality marijuana that is often made 'better' by adding other drugs to it," Zeese said. "And often the other drugs are more dangerous than the marijuana is. And the kids don't know that.... The government has no control over that either. But if they had a regulatory system, they would have control over the purity.... Even if the kids got marijuana under legalization, they'd at least get safer marijuana."

Pot Cultivation Big Business in U.S.

The sale of marijuana has become a big business in the United States. According to the U.S. Drug Enforcement Administration (DEA) the retail value of imported and domestically grown marijuana was between $15.5 and $21.9 billion in 1979, the last year for which complete statistics are available.[20]

---

[19] Quoted in *The Washington Star*, July 10, 1981.
[20] See DEA's National Narcotics Intelligence Consumers Committee report, "The Supply of Drugs to the U.S. Illicit Market from Foreign and Domestic Sources in 1979." The average retail price of marijuana in the United States is about $40 an ounce; the strongest marijuana sells for up to $125 an ounce.

NORML estimates that the retail value of marijuana sales has reached $25 billion annually.

Retail sales of U.S.-grown marijuana amount to about $8.2 billion, making marijuana the fourth largest U.S. cash crop, behind soybeans ($13.3 billion), corn ($12.8 billion) and wheat ($8.99 billion).[21] Marijuana is the No. 1 cash crop in the nation's leading agricultural state, California. About one-fifth of all domestically grown marijuana is cultivated in California, primarily in the state's northern counties. California's marijuana crop is worth at least $1 billion annually. Marijuana also is the top cash crop in Hawaii, and is being cultivated commercially in at least 30, and possibly all 50, states.

In Virginia, law enforcement officials uncovered evidence of large-scale marijuana farming for the first time in 1981. Until then, Virginia narcotics agents found that most of the pot grown in the state was cultivated for personal use. But now, said Dennis W. Roberts of the State Police Narcotics Bureau, "they're growing it to sell. . . ." [22] Police estimate that the marijuana crops in Kentucky and Oklahoma each were worth about $200 million in 1981. "When I started, I found it difficult to believe it could be Kentucky's biggest cash crop," said Lt. Louis Stiles of the Kentucky State Police, "but I don't find that too hard to believe any more." [23]

High Cost of the Imported Varieties

One of the primary reasons for the growing domestic market is the high cost of imported marijuana, most of which now is shipped through southern Florida from Colombia, where some 100,000 acres are under marijuana cultivation. Most of the rest of the imported marijuana comes from Mexico and Jamaica. A decade ago Mexico was the prime supplier of U.S. marijuana, but that situation changed beginning in the early 1970s when the Mexican government, under pressure from the United States, started cracking down on the marijuana trade.

In the fall of 1975 Mexico began a marijuana crop-eradication program funded by the United States. The main weapon was aerial spraying with the herbicide paraquat. In March 1978 NORML filed suit to stop the paraquat spraying after a NIDA study found that paraquat-laden marijuana could cause permanent lung damage. The suit was denied by a federal judge, but many U.S. marijuana smokers learned of the possible hazards of Mexican marijuana. Perhaps because of the paraquat scare, or perhaps because of the effectiveness of the eradication program, Mexico's share of the U.S. pot market plunged. In 1976 Mexico

[21] U.S. Department of Agriculture figures for 1980.
[22] Quoted in *The New York Times,* Sept. 6, 1981.
[23] Quoted in *U.S. News & World Report,* Oct. 12, 1981, p. 63.

The U.S. Marijuana Market — 1980			
Country of Origin	Quantity (Metric Tons)	Percent of Total Imports	Percent of Total Supply
Colombia	7,700-11,300	81%	75%
Jamaica	1,000-1,400	10	10
Mexico	800-1,300	9	8
Domestic	700-1,000	—	7

Source: Drug Enforcement Administration

accounted for 70 percent of the U.S. supply; today the figure is about 8 percent.

Mexico's place as the prime U.S. supplier has been taken by Colombia, which now provides 75 to 80 percent of the U.S. marijuana supply. The U.S. government is now working with the Colombian government to reduce marijuana and cocaine exports. The United States has provided nearly $20 million in grants to Colombia in the last two years for anti-marijuana efforts. At home, three federal agencies — the Customs Service, the Coast Guard and the Drug Enforcement Administration — have joined together in "Operation Tiburon," a southern-Florida-based effort designed to stem the Colombia marijuana flow. Since the operation began early in 1980, U.S. authorities have arrested more than 500 marijuana smugglers and seized 95 boats. Some 6.5 million pounds of Colombian marijuana — about 20 percent of the total smuggled into the United States — was seized. From Dec. 1-17, 1981 (the beginning of the harvest season), the Customs Service made 26 seizures in southern Florida.

Colombia's National Police took over drug enforcement duties from that nation's Army in December 1980, and observers say this has had a positive impact on cutting back marijuana exports to the United States. "Since the first of January 1981, the National Police have deployed more than 1,000 men throughout the country in new anti-narcotics units, launching an increasingly effective interdiction campaign," John H. Linnemann, a U.S. State Department narcotics specialist, said in November 1981.[24] Clyde Taylor, a State Department expert on South American drug traffic, recently witnessed the Colombian police in action. "They use helicopters for reconnaisance, and they go out by helicopter to do seizures," Taylor said. "They transport it back or burn it on site, and destroy the facilities where they do the pressing. . . . [A]t one police depot, they burn 40 to 50 tons every week. We saw 45 tons burned."[25]

[24] Testifying before the Permanent Subcommittee of Investigation of the Senate Governmental Affairs Committee, Nov. 13, 1981. Linneman is deputy assistant secretary of the State Department's Bureau of International Narcotics Matters.
[25] Quoted in the Miami Herald, Dec. 26, 1981.

While Colombia's marijuana flow has slowed, no one is predicting the end of the Colombia pot pipeline, and the State Department is pushing to get continued U.S. aid for Colombia's anti-marijuana program.

Ongoing Debate Over Decriminalization

At home, the possession of marijuana for personal use has been decriminalized in 11 states *(see box, p. 79).*[26] Oregon led the way in 1973 when it reclassified possession of up to one ounce as a "violation" carrying a maximum penalty of a $100 fine. Twenty-seven other states now allow a conditional discharge for the first offense in possession cases. Despite these liberalized laws, it is still possible to serve a long prison sentence for a marijuana offense.

For example, on Jan. 11, 1982, the U.S. Supreme Court upheld a 40-year prison sentence imposed on a Virginia man, Roger T. Davis, for possession and distribution of nine ounces of marijuana worth some $200. And the Virginia General Assembly currently is considering legislation that would impose a mandatory sentence of from three to 10 years in prison and a fine of not less than $10,000 for someone convicted of having between 10 and 100 pounds of marijuana. About 400,000 persons nationwide were arrested last year for marijuana-related offenses; nearly 90 percent of the cases involved possession rather than sale of the drug. About 20,000 persons are currently in jail for marijuana offenses.

Reformers argue that criminal penalties should be removed because marijuana possession is a "victimless" crime that harms only the arrested person. A marijuana arrest can scar a person's life, hold back job opportunities or advancements and acceptances to schools. Marijuana reformers also say that the $3 billion a year spent on marijuana law enforcement could be used to fight other, more serious crimes. In California, state law enforcement authorities have saved an estimated $150 million in police and court costs since marijuana was decriminalized in 1975.[27]

The last state to decriminalized marijuana did so in 1978, and it does not appear likely that any others will enact liberalized measures in the near future. NORML believes that Michigan, Wisconsin and the District of Columbia are the three jurisdictions most likely to join the 11 states that have decriminalized marijuana. But observers do not expect any action during 1982, an election year.

---

[26] Decriminalization is not the same thing as legalization. Decriminalization laws define possession or use of small amounts of marijuana as a civil offense or minor misdemeanor subject to nominal fines. No criminal penalties are imposed.

[27] See National Organization for the Reform of Marijuana Laws, "Marijuana in America: The Facts," fall 1981.

The Decriminalization Picture

State	Year	Maximum Fine Imposed	Maximum Amount Possessed
Oregon	1973	$100	1 oz.
Alaska	1975	$100	Any amount in private for personal use or 1 oz. in public
Maine	1976	$200	Any amount for personal use
Colorado	1976	$100	1 oz.
California	1976	$100	1 oz.
Ohio	1975	$100	100 grams (approx. 3.5 oz.)
Minnesota	1976	$100	1.5 oz.
Mississippi	1977	$250	1 oz.
North Carolina	1977	$100	1 oz.
New York	1977	$100	25 grams (approx. 7/8 oz.)
Nebraska	1978	$100	1 oz.

Source: National Organization for the Reform of Marijuana Laws

While the government continues to take a hard line against marijuana, legal reforms in the not-too-distant future are possible. "The time is coming when a majority of Americans will have smoked, and there is every reason to think they will be more tolerant of marijuana than the present, non-smoking majority," said Patrick Anderson.[28] Even those who support stiffer penalties for marijuana possession or use admit that this approach may not necessarily cut down on the number of people who smoke marijuana. After all, Prohibition did not stop the use of alcohol. On the other hand, any evidence of a direct link between marijuana and serious health problems could lessen the popularity of the drug.

---

[28] Anderson, *op. cit.*, p. 319.

Selected Bibliography

Books

Anderson, Patrick, *High in America: The True Story of NORML and the Politics of Marijuana,* Viking, 1981.

Bonnie, Richard J. and Charles Whitead, *The Marijuana Conviction: A History of Marijuana Prohibition in the United States,* University of Virginia Press, 1974.

Brecher, Edward M., *et al., Licit and Illicit Drugs,* Consumers Union, 1972.

Drake, William Daniel Jr., *The Connoisseur's Handbook of Marijuana,* Straight Arrow Books, 1971.

Grinspoon, Lester, *Marijuana Reconsidered,* Harvard University Press, 2nd ed., 1975.

Kaplan, John, *Marijuana: The New Prohibition,* World Publishing, 1970.

Schroeder, Richard C., *The Politics of Drugs: An American Dilemma,* Congressional Quarterly, 2nd ed., 1980.

Snyder, Solomon H., *Uses of Marijuana,* Oxford University Press, 1971.

Weil, Andrew, *The Natural Mind,* Houghton Mifflin, 1972.

Articles

Brynner, Elisabeth Coleman, "New Parental Push Against Marijuana," *The New York Times Magazine,* Feb. 10, 1980.

Lang, John, "Marijuana: A U.S. Farm Crop That's Booming," *U.S. News & World Report,* Oct. 12, 1981.

"Marijuana — What are the Risks?" *The Harvard Medical School Health Letter,* June 1980.

Reports and Studies

Editorial Research Reports: "Changing U.S. Drug Policy," 1976 Vol. I, p. 45; "Marijuana and the Law," 1975 Vol. I, p. 123; "World Drug Traffic," 1972 Vol. II, p. 927; "Legalization of Marijuana," 1967 Vol. II, p. 577; "Psychotoxic Drugs," 1965 Vol. I, p. 63.

National Institute on Drug Abuse: "For Parents Only: What You Need to Know About Marijuana," 1981; "Marijuana and Health: Eighth Annual Report to the U.S. Congress from the Secretary of Health and Human Services," 1980.

National Narcotics Intelligence Consumers Committee, "The Supply of Drugs to the U.S. Illicit Market from Foreign and Domestic Sources in 1979," 1981.

National Organization for the Reform of Marijuana Laws, "Marijuana in America: The Facts," fall 1981.

SEX EDUCATION

by

Marc Leepson

Aug. 28
1 9 8 1

Editor's Note: Montana has joined Delaware, Iowa, Kansas, Minnesota, Pennsylvania and Utah in encouraging local school districts to offer sex education courses *(see p. 86)*, leaving only 18 states with no official policy on the matter.

SEX EDUCATION

SEX EDUCATION is one of the most controversial issues in American public education. Recent opinion polls indicate that a large majority of Americans approve of teaching sex education in public schools.[1] Yet such courses are mandatory only in New Jersey, Maryland and the District of Columbia. Even when sex education is provided in schools, birth control often is not discussed. Experts estimate that fewer than one-third of all U.S. public-school students are taking sex education courses that include instruction in contraception.

Unlike most school subjects, sex education deals with a sensitive, highly personal area of life — one that some parents believe should not be discussed in the classroom. These parents maintain that it is their responsibility — or that of their priest, minister or rabbi — to instruct their sons and daughters on sexual matters. Most opponents of sex education see nothing wrong with schools providing instruction in human biology and the "facts of life." What they object to is what they say are the unintended messages of many sex education programs: to encourage children to experiment with sex and to disregard traditional and religious moral teachings.

Sex education programs "constitute not instruction but indoctrination," said Jacqueline Kasun, a professor of economics at Humboldt State University and an opponent of sex education in schools. These programs teach "that any kind of sexual choice is perfectly all right and is up to the individual, provided only that it does not produce babies. And that includes homosexuality. It includes masturbation. It includes sex outside of marriage."[2]

Opposition to sex education is not limited to religious fundamentalists. Psychoanalyst and educator Bruno Bettelheim, for example, believes there is little that teachers can do to influence teen-agers in sexual matters. "In my opinion, sex education is impossible in a classroom," he said recently. "Sex

---

[1] A national survey conducted in May 1981 for *Time* magazine by the research firm of Yankelovich, Skelly and White found that 70 percent of those polled approved of sex education classes in public schools that included information on birth control; 25 percent disapproved. In a Gallup Poll released Jan. 23, 1978, 77 percent of those questioned said they thought sex education should be taught in schools and 69 percent said sex education courses should include instruction in contraception.

[2] Quoted in *U.S. News & World Report*, Oct. 6, 1980, p. 89.

education is a continuous process, and it begins the moment you are born. It's in how you are bathed, how you are diapered, how you are toilet-trained, in respect for the body, in the notion that bodily feelings are pleasant and that bodily functions are not disgusting. . . . How you feel about sex comes from watching how your parents live together, how they enjoy each other's company, the respect they have for each other. . . . The problem in sex is sexual anxiety, and you cannot teach about sexual anxiety because each person has different anxieties."[3]

Scott Thompson, executive director of the National Association of Secondary School Principals, agrees with Bettelheim. Thompson believes sex education will not help decrease the number of teen-age pregnancies nor cut back on the spread of venereal disease among young persons because these are "matters of attitudes and values and outlooks." "Most high school people have been so well inoculated with the attitudes and values of films, publications, rock music and television programs . . . ," Thompson said in a recent interview, "that by the time they are 14 or 15 years old, any attempt on the part of the schools to counsel caution . . . or even to teach something in the way of birth control, is really not going to be that effective or have that much impact on what happens. . . ."[4]

Thompson maintains that sex education in secondary schools is a waste of money. "We shouldn't be throwing our money away on these kinds of efforts," he said, "because they are not going to have any impact. Let's spend our money on things that schools can teach like writing and reading, music and art. We can do that. We can't teach kids not to play around — given the society that we're in."

Arguments in Favor of Sex Education

Those in favor of sex education classes in public schools say that it provides young people with knowledge that could help bring down the alarming rate of teen-age pregnancy *(see p. 90)*. "If nothing else, just by giving young people a better notion of the risk of pregnancy that's involved and giving them accurate information and referral to services where they can get contraception, sex education certainly ought to do something to keep down the pregnancy rate," Richard Lincoln, senior vice president of the Alan Guttmacher Institute, told Editorial Research Reports.[5]

Peter Scales, director of the National Study on Barriers to Sex Education, contends that the goals of sex education go

---

[3] Interview with Elizabeth Hall in *Psychology Today*, July 1981, p. 40.
[4] The National Association of Secondary School Principals is located in Reston, Va.
[5] The Alan Guttmacher Institute, a research and analysis corporation, is affiliated with Planned Parenthood.

Sex education deals with a sensitive, highly personal area of life.

beyond helping avoid unwanted pregnancies and venereal disease. "Sex education should be approached not as a solution to a problem, but as a natural response to an irrefutable need," he said. "It provides young people with the skills to make choices in a world that is far more socially complex than the one their parents had to deal with."[6] Scales believes that religious training and parental information about sex often are inadequate. "It's fine and good when young people find firm guidance in religious teachings and in what parents have told them," he said, "but communication between parents and their children on sexual matters is typically characterized by evasiveness and embarrassed silence. Also, kids these days don't get all their values and information from parents and church, if they ever did. They get them from television, from records, from their friends, from public school bathrooms — you name it."

Some of those who support sex education generally believe that the subject is not suited for every school. "Sex education is appropriate in schools where morale is high, where students are enthusiastic and involved. In such an emotionally reinforcing environment, schools may be able to help adolescents develop a better awareness of their own sexuality as well as a greater sensitivity to others," wrote Syracuse University Professor Sol Gordon. "But in schools where morale is low and students are generally apathetic, it is doubtful that a course in sex education can have a positive influence.... Among students who are gen-

---

[6] Quoted in *U.S. News & World Report*, Oct. 6, 1980, p. 89.

erally apathetic and clearly 'turned off,' traditional sex education designed to influence attitudes and sexual behavior is not likely to produce significant results."[7]

Different State Policies on the Issue

According to a Gallup Poll released Oct. 4, 1978, about 43 percent of students aged 13-18 reported having had any sex education in school. But only 31 percent of that group said they were taught about contraception. A 1979 study conducted by Professor Melvin Zelnik of Johns Hopkins University[8] indicated that two-thirds of female students aged 15-19 had some sex education courses in school; less than half said they had instruction in birth control methods. Ninety percent of those girls who received sex education said their courses included information about venereal disease; nearly all were taught about the menstrual cycle.

Maryland, New Jersey and the District of Columbia are the only jurisdictions that require local school boards to provide sex education instruction. Kentucky has a law requiring that sex education be offered as part of mandatory health classes but has no specific policy as to how the program should be implemented. Six states — Delaware, Iowa, Kansas, Minnesota, Pennsylvania and Utah — encourage, but do not mandate, local school districts to offer sex education courses. Twenty-two states leave the decision to the local school boards; the remaining 19 states have no official policy on the matter *(see map, p. 87)*. Michigan and Louisiana at one time had laws banning the teaching of sex education in schools. The Michigan law was repealed in 1977, the Louisiana law in 1979.

The New Jersey Board of Education in August 1980 ordered all of the state's school districts to set up sex education courses — called "family life" courses — by September 1983. The courses are to begin no later than the sixth grade and continue through high school. Local school districts will be permitted to draw up their schools' courses. Students may be excused from the classes if their parents wish. The school board's action spawned a debate in the New Jersey legislature. Among the groups lobbying against the order were the State Teachers Association, the State School Boards Association and the New Jersey Right to Life Committee. Among those favoring the measure were Planned Parenthood, the Junior League and the Roman Catholic Church.

The state teachers and school board associations opposed the

---

[7] Sol Gordon, *et al., The Sexual Adolescent* (1979), pp. 49-50.
[8] Melvin Zelnik, "Sex Education and Knowledge of Pregnancy Risk Among U.S. Teenage Women," *Family Planning Perspectives,* Vol. XII, 1980.

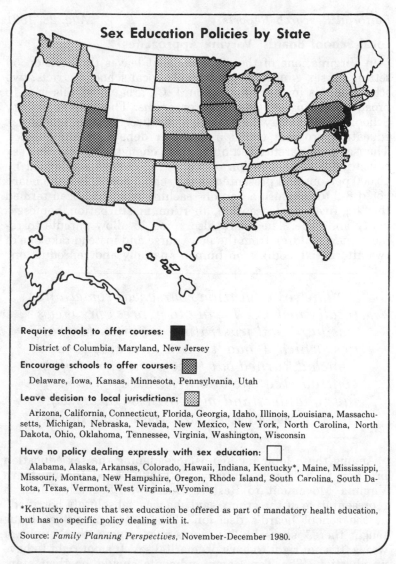

Sex Education Policies by State

Require schools to offer courses: ■

District of Columbia, Maryland, New Jersey

Encourage schools to offer courses: ▦

Delaware, Iowa, Kansas, Minnesota, Pennsylvania, Utah

Leave decision to local jurisdictions: ▒

Arizona, California, Connecticut, Florida, Georgia, Idaho, Illinois, Louisiana, Massachusetts, Michigan, Nebraska, Nevada, New Mexico, New York, North Carolina, North Dakota, Ohio, Oklahoma, Tennessee, Virginia, Washington, Wisconsin

Have no policy dealing expressly with sex education: ☐

Alabama, Alaska, Arkansas, Colorado, Hawaii, Indiana, Kentucky*, Maine, Mississippi, Missouri, Montana, New Hampshire, Oregon, Rhode Island, South Carolina, South Dakota, Texas, Vermont, West Virginia, Wyoming

*Kentucky requires that sex education be offered as part of mandatory health education, but has no specific policy dealing with it.

Source: *Family Planning Perspectives,* November-December 1980.

plan primarily because they felt sex education was an issue that should be handled solely by local school boards. Others opposed the plan because they did not believe sex education should be taught in public schools. The state's Right to Life Committee objected to the program because the school board's guidelines allowed abortion to be taught as an alternative to childbirth. The New Jersey Assembly on June 11 turned back an attempt to overturn the school board order when it voted down a bill that would have prohibited any state agency from ordering local school boards to have sex education programs. Opponents of sex education say they will continue to challenge the ruling in the coming months.

Local School Boards' Varying Approaches

In Virginia, one of the 22 states that leaves the decision on setting up sex education programs to local school districts, two school boards in the Washington, D.C., area voted this year to broaden existing sex education programs. The Fairfax County School Board's May 14 vote to liberalize its high school sex education program ended a five-year debate on the subject. Thousands of parents had objected to changing the existing sex education plan. A petition opposing the change was signed by 10,000 persons and presented to the school board. But the board voted 8-2 to overturn a ban on teaching what had been termed the "big five": contraception, abortion, masturbation, homosexuality and rape. The board also voted to allow parents to remove their children from the new course and instead take one of two alternative courses on human anatomy and reproduction.

"The sex education course was something totally new.... Trying to express my views was hard and frustrating at times. My values, which I had thought were solid and ironclad, turned out to be unsure, and often contradicted one another. It was great trying to understand myself through myself."

Massachusetts high school senior (female)

Among those lobbying against broadening the sex education program in Fairfax County was a group called the Northern Virginia Movement to Restore Decency. Elizabeth Burch, a representative of the group, said she was "absolutely horrified" at the school board's decision. "There are no values being taught there," she said. "Students won't know what's right or wrong. It's not right to have premarital sex. It's not right to have an abortion. The Ten Commandments should be their standards."[9] The school board's action came after a survey indicated that 75 percent of the county's parents favored expanding the sex education program in the schools.

On June 24 the Alexandria, Va., school board voted unanimously to direct the county's school staff to begin working on a curriculum for sex education courses. The new courses, which will begin in September 1982, will cover not only the "big five," but also child rearing, the integrity of the family, divorce and making "responsible choices" about sex. Contrary to the experience in neighboring Fairfax County, the Alexandria school

---

[9] Quoted in *The Washington Post*, May 15, 1981.

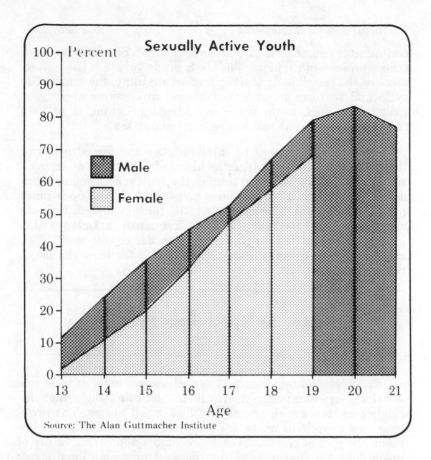

Sexually Active Youth

Percent

100
90
80
70
60 — Male
50 — Female
40
30
20
10
0

13   14   15   16   17   18   19   20   21

Age

Source: The Alan Guttmacher Institute

board's action came without acrimonious debate. The main reason, officials said, was that the school board worked closely with parent groups in studying the issue and formulating the basis for the new program.

Education experts point to sex education programs in Flint, Mich., and Falls Church, Va., as among the most successful in the nation. The Flint Family Life Education Program begins in grade four, when students study the facts of reproduction. In grades 10-12, the program concentrates on "psycho-social and psycho-sexual concepts." The entire program tries to help students develop a system of values to help them with decisions about sex. It encourages participation by parents, including instruction to help parents communicate with their children on sexual matters.

The Falls Church program also involves parents. Among other things, the school system sponsors seminars for parents in which they learn the program's details. The program — which is optional for students — consists of a year-long Life Sciences course for sixth graders, another course for ninth graders and a one-quarter course called Seminar on Human Sexuality for high school juniors and seniors. The sixth-grade course is the center-piece of the program. It teaches human anatomy, the human life cycle and features no-questions-barred discussions about sexuality. The goal, as in the Flint, Mich., program, is to help teenagers make responsible decisions about sex.

"The kids are exposed to so much aberrant sexual behavior that sex education counteracts this media blitz we're seeing," said Mary Lee Tatum, who teaches the high school senior seminar in Falls Church. "The course gives the kids an opportunity to talk about something more than the fantasy images they see constantly." Tatum said the most frequently asked question from students is, "How can I get him or her to like me?" They are curious about sex, she said, "but that is far from the major topic of interest."[10]

Problem of Teen-Age Pregnancy

A dvocates and opponents of sex education have at least one thing in common: concern about the alarmingly high in-cidence of teen-age pregnancy in the United States. The prob-lems are especially acute for pregnant, unmarried girls. For them, the joys of childbirth often become a depressing future of unemployment, poverty, welfare dependency, emotional stress and health problems for mother and child.[11] For married teen-agers — both mother and father — the birth of a child abruptly signals the end of youth and the beginning of adult responsibil-ities, an experience described by rock musician Bruce Springsteen:

> Then I got Mary pregnant
> And, man, that was all she wrote
> And for my 19th birthday I got a union card
>   and a wedding coat
> We went down to the courthouse
> And the judge put it all to rest
> No wedding day smiles, no walk down the aisle,
> No flowers, no wedding dress
>
> — "The River," © 1979-80 by Bruce Springsteen,
>   used by permission

In 1978, the last year for which complete statistics are avail-able, some 1.1 million girls aged 15-19 became pregnant; about

---

[10] Quoted in *The Washington Post*, April 4, 1981.
[11] See "Teen-age Pregnancy," *E.R.R.*, 1979 Vol. I, pp. 205-224.

540,000 actually gave birth. Of those births, 44.9 percent were out of wedlock. Some 29,500 girls below age 15 became pregnant in 1978; about 10,800 gave birth. More than one teen-age girl in 10 gets pregnant each year and, according to the Alan Guttmacher Institute, if patterns do not change, four in 10 of the girls who turned 14 in 1981 will have at least one pregnancy while still in their teens; two in 10 will give birth at least once. Some 1.3 million children now live with teen-age mothers — half of whom are unmarried. An additional 1.6 million children under age five live with mothers who were teen-agers when they gave birth.[12]

Those on both sides of the sex education debate also are concerned about the high rate of venereal disease among teen-agers. According to the federal Center for Disease Control, the incidence of gonorrhea — the No. 1 reportable communicable disease in the United States — is nearly three times higher among teen-agers than among the general population. In 1979, the last year for which complete statistics are available, the gonorrhea rate for boys and girls aged 15-19 was 1,211.4 per 100,000 population, compared to the general population rate of 459.4. The rate of primary and secondary syphilis for teen-agers was 16.2 per 100,000 population; for all ages the rate was 11.4 *(see box, p. 94)*. These figures represent reported VD cases, but medical authorities say that hundreds of thousands of cases of gonorrhea and syphilis go unreported each year.[13]

Questions About Value of Sex Education

While it is argued that teen-age pregnancy and venereal disease are serious problems, there is no agreement on what to do about them. Most sex education advocates say that the best way to prevent teen-age pregnancy and venereal disease is to provide pertinent information in sex education classes. Sex education proponents also advocate providing social services to unwed teen-agers through government-financed family planning centers.

Opponents of sex education, on the other hand, say that teaching about sex in schools and helping teen-agers with birth control and family planning are not only the wrong answers to the problem, but, in fact, contribute to the problem. Connaught Marshner, president of the Pro-Family Coalition, an organization that represents some 100 state and local family-oriented groups, says that sex education proponents ignore the "root cause of the escalation of teen-age pregnancy, which is promiscuity." Marshner believes that sex education courses and family

[12] Statistics from the Alan Guttmacher Institute, "Teenage Pregnancy: The Problem That Hasn't Gone Away," March 1981.
[13] See "Venereal Disease: Continuing Problem," *E.R.R.*, 1979 Vol. I, pp. 45-64.

planning centers foster "indiscriminate sex" among teen-agers. Why are teen-agers having indiscriminate sex? "Because they have been cultivated in a mindset, in a mentality, that anything goes," Marshner said, "and that abstinence is not an acceptable alternative, and this is the promiscuity mindset."[14]

Those favoring sex education say that it has not been proven that such instruction puts "ideas" in teen-agers' heads. "There has been no evidence that sex education has had any effect on sexual activity," Richard Lincoln of the Alan Guttmacher Institute told Editorial Research Reports. "The few studies that there have been have shown that it has no effect. It hasn't increased it; hasn't decreased it. There has not been a national study of the subject so there's no way of definitely answering that question." Lincoln added: "Theoretically, I would think that a better informed young person is better able to resist exploitative sex and to make more rational decisions about sexual activity and resist the pressures than one who is poorly informed. But I think ... it [sex education] probably has very little effect on sexual activity."

Debate in Congress on Family Planning

The argument over the merits of sex education parallels the recent debate in Congress on the future of the only federal government agency that provides family planning services, the Office for Family Planning in the Department of Health and Human Services. The office provides funds that help finance some 5,100 family planning counseling centers throughout the country and another 27 centers that focus primarily on pregnant teen-agers and parents under age 18. Congress set up the larger program a decade ago under Title X of the Public Health Services Act of 1970. The counseling centers, which provided services to some 4 million women last year, give physical examinations and birth control advice that includes referral service for abortion. The teen-age counseling program was begun three years ago to try to deal with the rising numbers of teen-age pregnancies. In the current fiscal year family planning will receive some $162 million in federal funds.

The first salvo in the war of words over the government's role in family planning and sex education came Jan. 29 when Health and Human Services Secretary Richard S. Schweiker told a news conference in Washington, D.C., that he believed sex education was primarily a responsibility of parents. "I don't think it's the fed's role to do it," he said, "and I don't think it's the state's role unless the local school agency does it with the express approval of the parent." Schweiker later explained to the House Ways and Means Committee that he did not want to

---

[14] Appearing on "The MacNeil/Lehrer Report," PBS-TV, June 23, 1981.

do away with governmental family planning support but that he was against having the government directly involved. "I support family planning per se," he told the panel Feb. 25. "The point I was trying to make was I didn't think the government should completely supplant the family in this operation and push them aside."

A congressional challenge to the teen-age family planning centers came this year from freshman Sen. Jeremiah Denton, R-Ala., who sponsored a bill that as originally drafted called for the promotion of teen-age "chastity" as a solution to "the problem of adolescent promiscuity." The bill originally defined "promiscuity" as "having sexual intercourse out of wedlock," but that language was left out of the final version, approved by the Senate Labor and Human Resources Committee June 24 and ultimately accepted by a House-Senate conference committee July 28.

"I have positive and negative feelings about the sex education course I took in high school. It was difficult to discuss sex in the open. . . . But looking back on it, I think it was more valuable than I thought at the time. . . . Many of the things I learned there I would not have learned at all or would have been learned from sources that wouldn't have been accurate."

New Jersey college senior (male)

Denton's measure provides federal funds for family planning but with the goal of promoting "self-discipline" among teen-agers. It continues funding the 27 centers that aid pregnant adolescents but also funds an as-yet-unspecified number of other educational centers designed to reach teen-agers before they become sexually active. The aim, an aide to Sen. Denton said, is to encourage teen-agers that "it is OK to say 'no.' "[15] Denton's bill was accepted by House and Senate conferees over the vehement objections of Rep. Toby Moffett, D-Conn., who called the new organizations "store-front chastity centers." Moffett said: "We're going to be laughed out of every junior high school in America for being irrelevant."

At the July 28 House-Senate reconciliation conference that discussed the measure, Moffett asked why Denton and other conservatives wanted to get the government into the business of counseling on sexual mores. Denton responded: "We are now teaching them to say 'yes' with government money. This bill is

---

[15] See Congressional Quarterly's *Weekly Report*, Aug. 1, 1981, p. 1388.

Teen-Age Venereal Disease Rates*

Gonorrhea

Year	Boys, Ages 10-14	Girls, Ages 10-14	Total, Ages 10-14	Boys, Ages 15-19	Girls, Ages 15-19	Total, Ages 15-19
1979	22.2	79.7	50.4	956.6	1,468.8	1,211.4
1978	22.8	76.8	49.3	977.6	1,481.7	1,228.9
1975	21.1	74.4	47.2	1,121.5	1,462.4	1,292.2
1969	17.5	25.7	21.5	895.8	532.4	712.5

Syphilis**

Year	Boys, Ages 10-14	Girls, Ages 10-14	Total, Ages 10-14	Boys, Ages 15-19	Girls, Ages 15-19	Total, Ages 15-19
1979	.4	1.2	.8	18.0	14.4	16.2
1978	.6	1.0	.8	16.5	12.7	14.6
1975	.7	1.5	1.1	18.3	17.7	18.0
1969	.7	1.4	1.1	18.1	19.7	18.9

*Per 100,000 population
**Primary and secondary syphilis.
Source: Center for Disease Control

intended to offer an alternative organizational setup." Denton and cosponsor Sen. Orrin G. Hatch, R-Utah, were supported by anti-abortion groups that are unhappy with the federal involvement in family planning.

Congress wound up authorizing the adolescent program at $30 million for each of the next three years. Of the money appropriated, one-third can be spent on "scientific research on the causes and consequences of premarital adolescent sexual relations and pregnancy." Of the remaining funds, two-thirds, or up to $13.3 million, can be spent on continuing the existing counseling center program to provide prenatal care and nutrition counseling to pregnant teen-agers. The final portion of the funding, up to $6.6 million, will go to prevention services, which will be provided by maternity homes, YWCAs and others who now operate programs for pregnant teen-agers, or by charitable or religious organizations not now involved.

The bill, as originally drafted by Sen. Denton, prohibited any reference to abortion during counseling sessions funded under the program. But the reconciliation conferees modified that restriction so information about abortion now will be provided if a teen-ager and her parents request it. The new program's primary thrust will be to promote adoption as a "positive option" for pregnant teen-agers. In order to receive counseling under the program, a teen-ager will have to have parental consent, although such permission will not be needed for testing for pregnancy or venereal disease. Counseling about contraception will continue to be allowed. Actual services, such as the provision of contraceptive devices, though, will be authorized only if not available in the community. Finally, parental permission will not be required in the current program, which also allows discussion of abortion as one of many options for pregnant teen-agers and provides contraceptive services.

One reason liberal members of Congress agreed to Denton's proposal was a compromise with conservatives over the issue of how to fund the larger 5,100-center family planning program. Conservatives, led by Sen. Hatch, had pushed to give the states responsibility for distributing funds as part of block grants authorized by Congress. That move, liberals said, would have effectively killed the program because many states would have used the money to fund other, less controversial programs. In agreement for passage of the Denton bill, Hatch and other conservatives dropped the proposal to put the Title X funds under the state block grant program.

Impact of 'Secular Humanism'

THE CONTROVERSY over sex education is being played out against the backdrop of a larger debate over the issue of secular humanism. In recent years fundamentalist Christian leaders such as the Rev. Jerry Falwell of the Moral Majority have led a campaign against secular humanism, which they characterize as an anti-Christian, anti-family ideology that has spread throughout American society. "Secular humanism has become the religion of America," Falwell said. It has "taken the place of the Bible."[16] Anti-humanists see sex education as incorporating the worst of humanism's tenets. Falwell, whose headquarters is in Lynchburg, Va., has described sex education as "academic pornography."

In its simplest form, humanism is a philosophy centered on human interests and values in which humans and their capabilities are the central concerns. "Man is the measure of all things," said Protagoras, a fifth century B.C. Greek philosopher, who historians believe first asserted the humanist position. Modern humanism has evolved through a broken and diverse route from the Renaissance, when humanism was a literary and intellectual movement concerned with ancient Greek and Roman classical studies — the humanities. "Gradually the old classical conception of man as an autonomous, independent, rational human being began to be revived," wrote historian W. Y. Jones of

---

[16] Quoted in *Newsweek*, July 6, 1981, p. 48. See also James David Besser, "Anti-Humanism on the Air," *The New Republic*, July 25, 1981, pp. 22-23.

Renaissance humanism. "That long forgotten appreciation of
the value and dignity of the human personality ... so long
buried under the weight of Christian humility and other-
worldliness, now re-emerged."[17]

Today the term "secular humanism" has been coined to de-
scribe the philosophy of a group of people, mainly writers,
scholars and educators, who reject supernatural religious beliefs
and emphasize science and reason. A "Secular Humanist Dec-
laration" issued last year by 61 humanists declared: "Men and
women are free and are responsible for their own destinies and
... they cannot look toward some transcendental being for
salvation." The American Humanist Association and the Ethical Culture Society (the two main humanist groups) have an
estimated 10,000 members.

Link Between Humanism and Sex Education

Opponents of secular humanism say that one of the ways in
which that philosophy is spread is through sex education
courses. Syndicated columnist Joseph Sobran is among those
who share this view. "Liberal sex education" automatically includes a "certain set of values [that is] more or less covertly
superordinated over the traditional ones," he wrote. These values include the belief that "casual sex is not only permissible, it
is virtually imperative." Sobran believes that sex education
should be undertaken by parents and religious teachers and
that sex education courses in schools constitute a usurpation of
the parents' rightful role.[18]

Scott Thompson of the National Association of Secondary
School Principals also believes that sex education instruction
wrongfully takes over family responsibilities. "Any policy that
allows my daughter, for example, to have an abortion without
my knowledge I'm firmly against because I think it erodes the
family," Thompson said in a recent interview. "Any policy that
allows a minor to make any decision along these lines without
the information of the family certainly undercuts the family and
destroys the family relationship. I am very much opposed to
that kind of interference in family relationships by volunteer
organizations or the state."

Other opponents of sex education and secular humanism are
even more outspoken. Humanists are "promoting sexual perver-
sion," declared pastor Lee Wine of Ashland, Ore., in an Aug. 21,
1980, radio broadcast over station KDOV-AM. They are doing
this because "they want to create such an obsession with sex

[17] W. Y. Jones, *A History of Western Philosophy* (1955), p. 57. See also "The New
Humanism," *E.R.R.*, 1970 Vol. II, pp. 813-832.
[18] Writing in *The Human Life Review*, winter 1981, pp. 97, 98.

among our young people that they will have no time for interest in spiritual pursuits. . . . So what do we have? Humanist obsessions: sex, pornography, marijuana, drugs, self-indulgence, rights without responsibility."

Groups Monitoring TV Shows and Books

In addition to their fight against sex education, the anti-humanists have been active in other related areas. For example, a television watchdog group in Tupelo, Miss., the National Federation for Decency, recently announced plans to monitor "The Phil Donohue Show," an award-winning television talk show, because the group claims the program concentrates too much on sex. "Never before in television history have we had a sex activist broadcaster such as Phil Donohue," the organization said in a press release issued Aug. 1. "Approximately two out of three of his shows are sex shows, and most of these promote abnormal sex, which Mr. Donohue prefers to call 'sexual alternatives.' Such shows have a mind-warping effect on youth and adults."

Anti-humanist groups also are challenging library books, textbooks and courses of study they consider anti-family, anti-American and anti-religion. In the libraries, the focus is on material that influences children to adopt immoral or secular humanistic attitudes. This is nothing new. Parents have been objecting to what they consider too much emphasis on non-traditional values for years.[19] But what is new is the extent of today's protests.

The American Library Association reported in December 1980 that there seemed to be an unprecedented number of complaints about books in public libraries following last year's presidential election. "In the past three or four years we have had an average of three to five complaints a week," said spokesman Judith Krug. "We are now averaging three to five complaints daily."[20] The association and two other groups — the Association for Supervision and Curriculum Development and the American Association of Publishers — conducted a survey before the election and found there was a large increase in the number of complaints received by libraries and schools in 1978-1980 compared to 1976-1978.

The survey, which was released July 31, found that about 75

[19] In 1974, for example, violent protests erupted in Kanawha County, W.Va., over the use of new textbooks that many parents regarded as anti-American, blasphemous, critical of parental authority, immoral and obscene. As a result of the controversy, the Kanawha school system placed parents on textbook selection committees and adopted special selection guidelines. During the 1970s, parental disputes with schools also arose in Hanover County, N.C., Baton Rouge, La., and in other parts of the country. See "Education's Return to Basics," *E.R.R.*, 1975 Vol. II, pp. 668-669.
[20] Quoted by United Press International in *The New York Times*, Dec. 11, 1980.

percent of the challenges to library and classroom materials were mounted by individual parents representing only themselves. Those who challenged material on the state level, however, tended to be members of groups. "The state challenges were much more organized," Bob Doyle of the American Library Association said in a recent interview. "It wasn't just individuals objecting to a book, but rather it was a group. Of these challenges the majority centered on concerns with regard to sex or sexuality, obscenity, objectional language and those types of things." The survey found that in more than half the challenges "books or other materials either were restricted or censorship was imposed."[21]

In addition to the many local organizations and parent groups working to keep the schools and libraries free of secular humanist materials, there is a textbook reviewing "clearinghouse" in Longview, Texas. Mel and Norma Gabler started Educational Research Analysts two years ago to advise parents on how to recognize textbooks advocating humanist teachings — including evolution, negations of Christianity and sexual freedom.

Criticism of the Anti-Humanist Movement

The anti-humanist movement has its own vehement critics who claim that humanism is being used as a scapegoat for all the ills that have beset society. "I think secular humanism is a straw man," said Paul Kurtz, a philosophy professor at the State University of New York at Buffalo, and editor of *The Humanist* magazine. "They are looking for someone to blame."[22] Dorothy Massie of the National Education Association put it this way: "It's a pervasive campaign, an epidemic and a real attack on public education.... It's really a witch hunt, only now the witches are humanists."[23]

Charles Krauthammer, associate editor of *The New Republic* magazine, wrote recently that secular humanism has come to be "a handy catchall to evoke all the changes of the postwar American cultural revolution: challenges to traditional sexual morality, civil and parental authority, and religious orthodoxy; to work, family, neighborhood, and church, as Ronald Reagan puts it. Ultimately, it is a reaction to a decline in religious values."[24] In essence, Krauthammer wrote, the phenomenon can be explained as "conservatives opposing secularization and calling for a religious renewal." This is not a new concept, but blaming one single group is new, Krauthammer said, and "potentially dangerous."

---

[21] The survey was entitled, "Limiting What Students Shall Read: Books and Other Learning Materials in our Schools: How They are Selected and How They are Banned."
[22] Quoted in *The New York Times*, May 17, 1981.
[23] Quoted in *Newsweek*, July 6, 1981, p. 48.
[24] Writing in *The New Republic*, July 25, 1981, p. 23.

Sex Education

Krauthammer believes it is illogical to blame society's declining religious values on the small number of humanists and that those opposed to humanism have taken what "otherwise would have been a shadowy struggle against a 500-year-old historical trend — secularization — [and] transformed [it] into a crusade against a militant ideology controlled by a vanguard of party activists — the humanists. . . . A generation ago the pernicious sappers of our vital spiritual juices were called 'godless Communists.' Now they are 'secular humanists.' "

How much support does the movement against secular humanism have? National polls indicate that a majority of Americans do not agree with the anti-humanists' views on sex education, abortion and other controversial social issues. Although the nation has taken a conservative turn in recent years, the shift appears to be focused more on economic than on social issues. A recent poll conducted for *Time* magazine, and published in the June 1, 1981, issue, found that Americans want less government intrusion into their lives, favor increasing military strength and worry about the permissive and immoral values reflected in the media. But the poll also indicated that a majority of Americans favor the Equal Rights Amendment, oppose making abortions illegal and want strong gun control legislation. And 70 percent of the respondents approved of sex education in public schools.

A *Washington Post*-ABC News poll released June 13, found that of those who had heard or read about the Moral Majority, 43 percent generally disapproved of the organization's positions, while 37 percent approved. On social issues, 61 percent supported the Equal Rights Amendment, 74 percent said they approved of legalized abortions in most cases, two-thirds said they believed birth control devices should be made available to teen-agers and about half said there is nothing wrong with sexual relations between unmarried partners.

The national polls may indicate disfavor with the anti-humanists' positions on social issues and sex education in schools. But this does not mean that there likely will be an increase in the number of sex education courses in public schools in the near future. As long as the option of setting up sex education is left to local school boards — as it is in 48 states — there probably will be no widespread movement to institute new and expanded courses on sex education. The main reason, analysts say, is that most local school boards are conservative in nature and highly sensitive to criticism from parents. And sex education is one issue that usually elicits strong feelings from parents nearly everywhere in the country.

Selected Bibliography

Books

Gordon, Sol, Peter Scales and Kathleen Everly, *The Sexual Adolescent: Communicating with Teenagers about Sex*, 2nd ed., Duxbury Press, 1979.

Jones, Richard M., *Fantasy and Feeling in Education*, New York University Press, 1968.

Osofsky, Howard J., *The Pregnant Teenager*, Charles C. Thomas, 1968.

Pogrebin, Letty Cottin, *Growing Up Free: Raising Your Child in the 80s*, McGraw-Hill, 1980.

Read, Donald A., Sidney B. Simon and Joel B. Goodman, *Health Education: The Search for Values*, Prentice-Hall, 1977.

Sorensen, Robert C., *Adolescent Sexuality in Contemporary America*, World, 1973.

Articles

Castleman, Michael, "Why Teenagers Get Pregnant," *The Nation*, Nov. 26, 1977.

Family Planning Perspectives, published by the Alan Guttmacher Institute, selected issues.

Horner, Constance, "Is the New Sex Education Going Too Far?" *The New York Times Magazine*, Dec. 7, 1980.

Krauthammer, Charles, "The Humanist Phantom," *The New Republic*, July 25, 1981.

"Our Children are Treated Like Idiots," interview with Bruno Bettelheim by Elizabeth Hall, *Psychology Today*, July 1981.

Pelham, Ann, "Conferees Vote Teen-Age Chastity Program," *Congressional Quarterly Weekly Report*, Aug. 1, 1981.

Sobran, Joseph, "Sex Education," *The Human Life Review*, winter 1981.

Reports and Studies

Alan Guttmacher Institute, "Teenage Pregnancy: The Problem That Hasn't Gone Away," 1981.

—— "Eleven Million Teenagers," 1976.

Editorial Research Reports: "Teen-Age Pregnancy," 1979 Vol. I, p. 205; "Venereal Disease: Continuing Problem," 1979 Vol. I, p. 45; "Sexual Revolution: Myth or Reality," 1970 Vol. I, p. 241; "The New Humanism," 1970 Vol. II, p. 813.

U.S. Center for Disease Control, "An Analysis of U.S. Sex Education Programs and Evaluation," July 1979.

Cover art by Staff Artist Cheryl Rowe; photo on p. 85
by Paul Conklin for Monkmeyer Press Photo Service

SHOPLIFTING

by

Jean Rosenblatt

Nov. 27
1981

SHOPLIFTING

HAVE YOU ever taken anything from a store without paying for it? If you did, you probably did not feel like a criminal. Shoplifting is a crime, but a small one when looked at as an isolated incident. Most shoplifters steal less than $30 worth of goods at a time. But in the aggregate, shoplifting costs retail stores and taxpayers billions of dollars a year. One study called shoplifting and employee theft "the most prevalent and (aside from organized crime) most costly crimes against business and society."[1]

According to the Atlanta-based National Coalition to Prevent Shoplifting, shoplifters cost Americans about $24 billion in 1980. This included the costs of security and prevention as well as the value of merchandise stolen, which is put at about $3 billion a year. Saul Astor, president of a New York City security company, estimates that one out of three small-business bankruptcies can be attributed to shoplifting and employee thefts.[2] Astor said shoplifting losses and the cost of extra security increase retail prices an average of 2 to 3 cents a dollar.

Precise estimates of shoplifting losses and even the number of people who shoplift are difficult to obtain, because, in the words of Gordon Williams, vice president for operations of the National Retail Merchants Association, "all you know is who you catch," and only about one out of 35 shoplifters is ever caught. Retailers base their loss estimates on shrinkage, the difference between their inventory and what they are supposed to have in stock. "It is the impression of the security managers in the department and specialty stores that are our members," Williams told Editorial Research Reports, "that shoplifting accounts for about 30 percent of their shortage; employee theft counts for about 40 percent; and the balance consists of errors and unrecorded markdowns."

Categories of People Tempted to Steal

Most experts divide shoplifters into three categories: the amateur, professional and kleptomaniac, someone with an un-

---

[1] Westinghouse Evaluation Institute, "National Evaluation Program — Phase I: Assessment of Shoplifting and Employee Theft Programs," 1979, p. 1. The institute, a division of Westinghouse Electronic Corp., was abolished in June 1981.
[2] Quoted in "Shoplifting Soars — And Merchants Strike Back," *U.S. News & World Report,* Dec. 3, 1979, p. 71.

controllable impulse to steal. Lawrence Conner, executive director of Shoplifters Anonymous, a pretrial rehabilitation program in Pennsylvania *(see p. 115),* believes there is a fourth type — the shoplifting addict. According to Conner, the addict steals more than the other three groups combined. He defined the shoplifting addict as "any non-criminal type, not stealing for resale, who has a habit ranging from once a day to once a month."[3] Over half (54 percent) of 1,300 participants in Shoplifters Anonymous surveyed over a three-year period admitted to stealing that often.

Of the shoplifting types, the kleptomaniac is the most rare. Professionals account for about 10 percent of all shoplifters, although according to some authorities that figure may merely indicate that professionals are more difficult to spot and apprehend. Professionals usually steal expensive items, use sophisticated methods like electronic jamming devices, and are skilled in manipulating and harassing store employees.

The most typical shoplifter is the amateur who steals on impulse for personal use. According to most studies, the greatest number are under age 21, with the peak age at about 15, although in some cities housewives and young women make up the largest group. The National Coalition to Prevent Shoplifting found that in more than half of the apprehensions they kept track of, shoplifters were between 13 and 19 years old. A 1979 study by the Westinghouse Evaluation Institute[4] said that one reason for the high number of young shoplifters may be that teen-agers are simply caught more often than other groups. The expectation that young people shoplift leads to closer surveillance, which could explain why more of them get caught. Younger shoplifters may also be less skilled at avoiding detection than older people. On the other hand, six out of seven students surveyed by the National Coalition to Prevent Shoplifting said they were never caught.

Many studies indicate that women shoplifters — at least those who are caught — outnumber men. One explanation is that women go shopping more often and the items they are most interested in, such as jewelry, cosmetics and clothing, are more accessible. But security personnel are quick to point out that shoplifters come from all age groups and backgrounds. According to Lewis Shealy, vice president of security at Woodward & Lothrop, a department store chain in the Washington, D.C., area, "in your better retail stores your shoplifter is your customer." Shoplifting does appear to be a middle-class phenomenon. According to security personnel involved in apprehen-

---

[3] Lawrence Conner, *The Shoplifters are Coming* (1980), p. 6.
[4] Westinghouse Evaluation Institute, *op. cit.,* p. 54.

sions, more than 90 percent of the people who are caught, including teen-agers, have enough cash or credit cards with them to pay for what they tried to steal.[5]

The peak seasons for shoplifting correspond to retailers' peak seasons for sales — Christmas and back-to-school time. More shoplifters are caught during these periods than any other times during the year. For this reason most anti-shoplifting campaigns are conducted between September and January. Security personnel also noticed a marked increase in shoplifting beginning in the early 1970s when inflation began seriously affecting consumers. Lewis Shealy said he found a significant rise in shoplifting in Washington, D.C., after the Watergate scandal in 1972. "People were really depressed," he said. "They thought everybody was stealing, so why shouldn't they? The next peak came during the energy crisis in the fall of 1974. This lasted for about a year, tapered off, picked up again in 1979 when gas prices started going up, and didn't taper off again until February 1980."

Psychological Motives for Retail Theft

Most people — if they have not actually lifted something — have thought about doing it. This is not surprising in a consumer society that constantly bombards people with the message that material possessions bring happiness, love and prestige. But aside fom society's materialistic emphasis, why do people other than kleptomaniacs shoplift? Security personnel seem to agree that shoplifters want something for nothing. Jack Lawrence, program director of Shoplifters Anonymous, explained the phenomenon this way: "It all revolves around 'I want.' People are drilled with media awareness of new products, and then they walk into these massive stores with all the rows of merchandise, and they decide to take a chance."[6]

In a Gallup youth survey conducted in October 1979, three-quarters of the 13-to-18-year-olds who admitted they had shoplifted said they did it for kicks. Most of the others said they did it on a dare or on impulse. Not having enough money for a desired item was the leading reason given by students surveyed by the National Coalition to Prevent Shoplifting. Several young women interviewed for a 1980 article in *Mademoiselle* magazine[7] said that excitement was a powerful motivator. "I just really liked the sly, furtive quality," said one woman. "There was something sexual about it — like doing it with your boyfriend before your parents come home." Another said,

---

[5] *Ibid.*, p. 57.
[6] Quoted by Gini Kopecky in "Shoplifting: Why Women Who Have Everything Steal," *Mademoiselle*, December 1980, p. 202.
[7] *Ibid.*, p. 156.

"There's a definite psychic charge to it. First, there is that awful fear of getting caught, then that wonderful feeling of not getting caught. It's just an incredible kick, a real high. It's almost like being on drugs."

Studies of women shoplifters have found that many were widowed or emotionally neglected by their husbands. The thrill of shoplifting was often an escape from monotony and depression and sometimes was sexually arousing. According to Alabama psychologist Esther Ann Beck, whether or not a woman experienced excitement often determined whether or not she would shoplift again.

George A. Furse, a psychotherapist and consultant to Shoplifters Anonymous, said that many of the shoplifters he has dealt with admitted to having other problems. Furse believes there is a large hostility component in shoplifting. "Many shoplifters, particularly the one-shot shoplifter, are really angry at something," he said in a recent interview. "Sometimes they're mad as hell at the store because prices are high, but very often you see displaced hostility against a spouse, the kids, the boss. . . . This kind of shoplifting is very impulsive."

But why do people pick shoplifting? "In a number of cases," Furse said, "people seem to be setting themselves up to get caught. The shoplifting is an indirect cry for help." He believes that the large number of shoplifters under age 19 and over age 45 supports the hostility theory, since hostility is the one thing shoplifters in both age groups have in common. "With kids it's more deliberate — a you-rip-us-off-so-we're-going-to-rip-you-off kind of thing," he said. "With older people the anger may be less conscious. Probably among younger people there is also more of an instant gratification component that you don't see as much in older folks."

George M. Harbin, senior vice president for marketing at Sensormatic Electronics Corp., a Florida company that makes and sells electronic security devices to retailers, explains shoplifting in terms of "a mental triangle that exists in everyone's mind." "One side of the triangle is frustration; two, opportunity; the third, low risk of getting caught," he said. "For most people, this triangle isn't usually connected. But it can trip into place anytime, anywhere, with anyone — and a person will steal."[8]

Modern Shoplifters Bred by Self-Service

"The city merchants are often subjected to heavy loss by professional shoplifters who throng their stores. The shoplifters

---

[8] Quoted in *Women's Wear Daily*, Sept. 15, 1976.

do not constitute the only thieves, however. Women of respectable position, led on by their mad passion for dress, have been detected in taking small but costly articles." This could be a description of what goes on in any big city today. But it actually describes conditions in New York City before the turn of the century.

Distinctions between shoplifting by amateurs, professionals and kleptomaniacs first began to be made in the late 19th century. Before then, Lawrence Connor wrote in *The Shoplifters are Coming* (1980), stealing from vendors was perpetrated primarily by "the hungry and the wicked." According to Connor, one event made shoplifting tempting to consumers of all types and backgrounds — the opening of a five and ten cent store in 1879 by Frank W. Woolworth. Woolworth was the first retailer to take merchandise out of glass cases and display it where customers could see it and touch it. He also put a price tag on each item and sold all merchandise for cash. The plan, intended to generate more sales with fewer employees, also increased the temptation to steal. As five and ten cent stores and self-service supermarkets became more popular, the prevalence of consumer theft rose.

Another difference between shoplifting before the days of self-service and after is the severity of punishment. At various times death, dismemberment, flogging, branding, imprisonment and public display have been inflicted on shoplifters. But over the years retailers began using a "warn and release" procedure. If they caught a shoplifter and retrieved the merchandise, they sometimes told the person never to return to the store rather than prosecute him.

Security expert Lewis Shealy believes the warn and release policy helped nurture the attitude that shoplifting was not a crime. "We wouldn't be in the position we are today if the retailer had taken a hard stand in the 1960s and early 1970s," he said. "They didn't want to admit they had a problem, and they didn't have security departments at that time." Today more stores have begun to prosecute shoplifters — an effective deterrent for first-timers, according to Shealy and others. More than 80 percent of the shoplifters caught in Washington, D.C., are prosecuted, up from less than 50 percent in the early 1970s.

Retailers' Anti-Theft Strategies

P ROSECUTION is an expensive and time-consuming process, costing up to $350 in employee time alone and taking up to six months. During that time merchandise has to be held as evidence and cannot be sold. And if there is no conviction, a retailer may face false-arrest charges. For these reasons many retailers prefer to deter their customers from shoplifting altogether. To this end they spend over half of 1 percent of their sales revenue on security management, including electronic surveillance devices, employee training programs, public awareness campaigns, security personnel and interior design strategies that minimize the opportunity to steal and facilitate surveillance. An increasingly large share of retailers' security expenditures is going to electronic devices, especially in big department stores. "With labor costs rising, retailers are able to justify the [expensive] electronic devices," said Gordon Williams of the National Retail Merchants Association.[9]

Surveillance has always been a big part of commercial security systems, but until recently it required the physical presence of security personnel. During the 1960s retailers began using closed-circuit television (CCTV) to extend the surveillance capabilities of their security staffs. Basically, CCTV in-

---

[9] Quoted in *Women's Wear Daily*, Jan. 7, 1980.

volves a fixed camera connected by cable to a monitor or display screen, providing a view of a specific area. There are several variations in the basic equipment, mostly in how the images are received (a stationary image or the panning of a wide area, for example) and how store personnel can change or control them.

The deterrent effect of CCTV is based on public knowledge that the system exists. To achieve this end, retailers place cameras in visible places, put up signs announcing the presence of cameras, place television screens connected to certain cameras throughout the store, or attach small strobe lights to the cameras to catch customers' attention. Retailers may also try to convince shoppers that they are under constant surveillance by using dummy cameras throughout a store, which also cuts costs.

Electronic article surveillance (EAS) is an anti-theft strategy that enables retailers to monitor tagged merchandise. The tags — usually large white pieces of plastic that theoretically can only be removed with special devices at the point of purchase — electronically activate an alarm whenever they pass through sensing screens placed near store or department exits. EAS proponents claim that it is a relatively sophisticated and cost-effective way to monitor a large amount of merchandise. "Not only is electronic article surveillance effective, but it's more cost-effective than a beefed-up security force because it allows you to operate with fewer employees and to make your remaining people more productive," said Bill Landres, vice president of loss prevention at the Hecht Co., a Washington, D.C., area department store chain. "Also, it enables you to pinpoint high-shoplifting areas within a store, such as a particular ladies' room or fitting area, that you might never know about otherwise."[10]

Electronic article surveillance works best when all items are tagged, when equipment is used properly and when store employees are trained to remove tags on every item sold and to properly approach someone who has caused an alarm to sound. The system is intended primarily as a deterrent, however, which is why its leading manufacturer, Sensormatic Electronics Corp., developed the highly visible white plastic tags. Originally the tags were hidden, with the result that an unmanageable number of thieves got caught, which also apparently caused some retailers embarrassment. For example, a system using hidden tags installed at a military PX caught the commanding officer's wife in its first week of operation. "They threw us right out," said Ronald G. Assaf, Sensormatic's founder.[11]

[10] Quoted in "The Difference Between a Systems Approach and a Methods Approach," *Security Management*, May 1981.
[11] Quoted in Peter Nulty, "Sensormatic Collars the Shoplifter," *Fortune*, Feb. 25, 1980, p. 115.

The use of electronic article surveillance seems to be increasing, although security experts report some problems with the system. Shoplifters sometimes are able to defeat the system by either removing the tag or shielding it with metal foil. There have also been problems with false alarms, which can result in false-arrest charges. In several reported cases retailers have paid cash to customers unfairly detained, searched or accused of shoplifting.

Involving Employees in Security Efforts

Many security experts agree with Lewis Shealy that electronic article surveillance "is a crutch that retailers use when they can't control shoplifting." According to Shealy, "beefing up a security force and pressing prosecutions are the way to go."[12] Woodward & Lothrop, where Shealy works, uses an arsenal of security techniques including store detectives, electronic and mechanical devices, participation in a local anti-crime campaign, a shoplifting "hotline" and the prosecution of more than 99 percent of the 3,000 or so people caught shoplifting there each year. "As far as we can determine," said Leonard Kolodny, manager of the Retail Bureau of the Greater Washington [D.C.] Board of Trade, "the retailers that prosecute regularly show more decreases in shoplifting than those who don't."

Lawrence Conner of Shoplifters Anonymous is among those who disagree with the claim of manufacturers of electronic article surveillance equipment that it is more cost-effective to watch merchandise than people. About 70 percent of the participants in Conner's program were caught with the help of some people-watching mechanical device — primarily closed-circuit television — and most were unaware that they were being watched while stealing. According to Conner, good security requires the active participation of everyone in a store, regardless of what devices are being used. Of the shoplifters he has interviewed, most said that being in the area of a uniformed guard made them too uncomfortable to shoplift. Advertising the use of plainclothes detectives also gives thieves the feeling that they can never be sure when they are being watched.

For these reasons, many retailers are putting more money into training programs that teach both security and non-security employees how to detect and respond to shoplifting. Employees are taught such things as how to spot and detain shoplifters, applicable state and local statutes and how to be an effective witness in court. Most programs emphasize the importance of the sales staff in preventing shoplifting, since prompt attention to customers reduces their frustration and perhaps

---

[12] Quoted in "The Difference between a Systems Approach and a Methods Approach," *Security Management,* May 1981.

Employee Theft

Employee theft is an even greater problem than shoplifting, accounting for annual losses of between $4 billion and $7 billion. Very few sticky-fingered employees get caught — about 3 percent, according to a 1973 survey of over 1,000 stores conducted by the Mass Retailing Institute. Of those caught, most are fired but only a few are prosecuted. Since the problem is so rampant, most retailers would rather pass on the cost of employee theft to consumers rather than use their resources to prosecute.

Employees take both merchandise and cash. One common method of stealing merchandise, security personnel say, is to leave items in trash or disposal areas to be picked up after hours. Like shoplifters, employees also use overcoats, shopping bags and lunch bags to conceal their loot, even though these items are usually forbidden in work areas. Often employees simply stash goods in their lockers. Retail workers may also misuse their discount privileges, report more hours than acutally worked, under-ring purchases or take cash out of the register.

their desire to steal. The success of these employee training programs has yet to be determined. According to security experts, many of them suffer from a lack of experienced teachers, insufficient educational materials and lack of understanding and support from top management.[13]

Informing the Public About Consequences

A number of organizations have sprung up in recent years to help combat shoplifting through public education. Judi Rogers, director of the Atlanta-based National Coalition to Prevent Shoplifting, says that such educational campaigns are necessary because "many individuals and institutions have developed a callous and indifferent attitude toward shoplifting that may actually encourage it to occur."[14] When Rogers first started looking into the problem over five years ago, she found that retailers as well as the public needed to be educated. "The big ones saw it [shoplifting] as a cost of doing business and were spending money on security . . . ," she said. "Many wouldn't prosecute; they were just happy to get their merchandise back."[15]

Since it was founded in September 1979, the coalition has tried to gain the cooperation of law enforcement officials and the courts to help ensure that shoplifters are not treated leniently. The organization also encourages retailers to prosecute those caught stealing from their stores.

---

[13] See Westinghouse Evaluation Institute, *op. cit.*, p. 140.
[14] National Coalition to Prevent Shoplifting, "Program Guide," 1981, p. 3.
[15] Quoted by Susan Percy in "Laying Down the Law on Shoplifting," *Atlanta Weekly*, Aug. 30, 1981, p. 48.

The National Retail Merchants Association encourges its members to participate in local anti-crime campaigns, which usually consist of seminars, lectures and media presentations, posters, signs, essay contests and advertising campaigns. The anti-crime campaign in Washington, D.C., considered the best in the country, is credited with reducing shoplifting in the area by 2 percent in the year ending July 31, 1981. This was the first time in the 12 years the Retail Bureau of the Greater Washington Board of Trade has been running the campaign that the figures had dropped. Last year the Washington campaign generated $2.8 million worth of public service advertising, making it the largest campaign in the country.

Besides placing posters in schools and public buildings, the Washington campaign relies heavily on school programs, billboards and radio and television advertising and talk show appearances by retailers, security personnel and law enforcement people. Newspaper ads mention the number of people arrested for shoplifting in a given week.[16] The campaign also provides a court sitting service for participating stores that alerts retailers a half hour before a shoplifting case is heard so the retailers or their employees will not have to wait around all day in court to testify. "In the last 12 years we've saved over 100,000 personnel hours which otherwise would have been wasted," program manager Leonard Kolodny told Editorial Research Reports.

Use of Criminal Justice System

THE LAWS governing shoplifting vary widely from state to state. In all but one state — Georgia — shoplifting is put in the category called retail theft or theft-by-taking.[17] "It is impossible in most states to find out how many people are even arrested for shoplifting because of the differences in how shoplifting is identified in states' criminal codes," Judi Rogers said in a recent interview.

To strengthen shoplifting laws and make them uniform, the National Coalition to Prevent Shoplifting has developed a model statute that among other things identifies shoplifting as an individual crime, defines what constitutes shoplifting and outlines how retailers should make apprehensions to avoid

---

[16] Between Sept. 21, 1980, and Jan. 4, 1981 — the duration of last year's campaign — 6,684 people were arrested for shoplifting in the Washington, D.C., metropolitan area.

[17] Georgia law has a separate category called "theft by shoplifting." Under the law, jail sentences are mandatory for second and subsequent offenses.

false-arrest suits. "We have no idea how many retailers are sued for false arrest, because they won't talk about it," Rogers said. "Retailers get into trouble when they drop a case and figure an arrest is enough because they don't want to spend the money and time to prosecute. [But] that's when a person turns around and sues them."

The fear of false-arrest suits and the difficulty retailers see in establishing "probable cause" — that is, that the suspect intended to steal — are major reasons why the ratio of prosecuted cases to shoplifting apprehensions is so low, the Westinghouse Evaluation Institute reported. But these concerns may be exaggerated. Every state but Rhode Island has a law that enables retailers to stop a suspect and question, search and detain him in a "reasonable manner" for a "reasonable time."[18] In most states it is not necessary to wait until the person suspected of shoplifting leaves the store before detaining him to establish an intent to steal. It is usually enough to observe concealment and recover the goods, either from the person or from where he stashed them before getting caught. If the goods are not recovered, however, it can be difficult to establish probable cause.

Private security guards cannot make arrests but can only detain a shoplifter until a police officer arrives.[19] Although guards are supposed to be well versed in what they can and cannot do, a survey of private security guards conducted by the National Institute of Law Enforcement and Criminal Justice found that 18 percent had no idea of their legal powers, 23 percent were unsure and 5.5 percent believed they could arrest suspects.

Leonard Kolodny, manager of the Washington, D.C., anti-crime campaign, says that while all a guard can legally do is search and interrogate, this experience alone can be terrifying to an amateur shoplifter. "The average person who steals from a retail store is unprepared to accept the consequences, and the mere stopping of a person — bringing a person into a special section of the store — that's a very traumatic experience," he said. "Being interrogated by security personnel scares away a lot of people."

Lawrence Conner advises retailers not inclined to prosecute to at least wait a while before they tell an apprehended shoplifter whether or not he will be prosecuted. "When typical non-

---

[18] Only five states explicitly define a reasonable time. In West Virginia, Maine and Montana a shoplifter can be held no longer than 30 minutes. In Indiana and Louisiana the maximum period is an hour.

[19] The California Supreme Court ruled Nov. 5, 1981, that private security guards in that state do not have to warn the suspects they detain of their constitutional rights to silence and legal counsel — the warning regular police officers must give under the so-called Miranda rule.

professional shoplifters are caught stealing merchandise, they have only one thing in mind," Conner wrote.[20] "They want to avoid prosecution and everything they say and do is geared toward achieving this objective. . . . They are hoping and praying they will hear the magic words 'If we ever catch you doing this again . . . ,' or 'Get out of this store and never come back.' The words may vary but . . . after they are spoken, the shoplifter walks out the front door experiencing an overwhelming sense of relief. In most cases, this gratifying emotional experience is so strong it overrides all negative aspects of the preceding trauma."

Ways of Handling Retail Theft in Court

Many retailers are cynical about the courts' value in controlling shoplifting. The backlog of cases, the amount of employee time tied up in court proceedings, the idiosyncratic treatment of cases by presiding judges and the insignificant penalties given have created a sense of futility among retailers. For their part, the courts generally find shoplifting cases a nuisance and, unless the shoplifter is a repeat offender, usually dismiss the case or order him or her to pay a light fine.[21]

Several strategies have been developed to improve the handling and disposition of shoplifting cases. A special shoplifting court in Chicago was designed "to reduce the time store security personnel and witnesses have to spend in court, save police resources by eliminating the need for police witnesses in misdemeanor cases and encourage more severe sentencing by eliminating the alternating of shoplifting cases with seemingly more serious cases before the same judge. The latter practice is thought to create an attitude among judges that shoplifting doesn't matter, and . . . doesn't warrant severe penalties."[22] These objectives have been accomplished by group docketing and processing shoplifting suspects in batches. Although there is no evidence yet that this procedure is effective in controlling shoplifting, reporting of shoplifting has increased significantly.

Court sitting programs like the one operated by the Greater Washington Board of Trade are being run by several local chambers of commerce and retail associations. These programs provide court liaison officers who monitor court dockets so they can notify a retailer who has a case pending when it will be tried. Retailers find these programs worth the $10 to $15 per case they usually have to pay, since they save much more than that in personnel hours that otherwise would have to be spent in court.

---

[20] Conner, *op. cit.*, p. 68.
[21] According to the Westinghouse Evaluation Institute study less than 5 percent of defendants receive a fine or a jail sentence.
[22] Westinghouse Evaluation Institute, *op. cit.*, p. 33.

Civil remedies for shoplifting — to both reimburse retailers for damages and deter shoplifters from future stealing — are becoming more common, especially since 14 states have enacted specific civil statutory penalties.[23] Under these statutes a retailer can demand a monetary payment from a shoplifter by putting the demand in writing. Civil actions can be brought against shoplifters who are not arrested or prosecuted. But most often retailers ask for damages in conjunction with arrests. This is because the evidence and arrest record that go along with an arrest increase the chance of a successful civil suit.

Value of Pretrial Rehabilitation Programs

Several communities divert accused and arrested shoplifters into rehabilitation programs. If the programs are completed, participants — usually first-time offenders — have their cases dismissed. Such factors as a defendant's past criminal record, his age, the value of the merchandise stolen, the sophistication of his methods and the retailer's desire to prosecute are taken into account when deciding whether to place someone in a rehabilitation program.

The Philadelphia Service Institute Program for Retail Theft Offenders has enrolled about 6,000 people since its first class was held in November 1978.[24] Direct referrals from merchants now make up about 30 percent of the participants. Police officers in that city have asked merchants to refer first offenders to the program in place of having them arrested. The program lasts about five hours and uses principles and techniques of guided group interaction, teaching, values clarification and group psychotherapy. It also includes a mock trial that is designed to teach participants that retailers have considerable power under the law and that "guilt or innocence is to be judged by the law and not by subjective feelings ... as to whether the merchant or the law is 'fair.' "[25]

Shoplifters Anonymous, in Aston, Pa., is a voluntary program for first offenders, whose applications must be reviewed and accepted by the police department, district court, program director and the retailer who caught the shoplifter. About three-quarters of the people who apply are accepted and of those, half complete the program successfully. Participants pay a $50 tuition fee to take part in the six-hour Saturday course. Shoplifters Anonymous recently developed a home-study course using cassette tapes. These courses are not limited to first offenders. The courses are not moralistic, but instead focus on the fact

---

[23] These states are Alaska, Arizona, California, Idaho, Illinois, Indiana, Nevada, New Mexico, North Dakota, Ohio, Utah, Vermont, Virginia and Wasington.
[24] The non-profit organization is housed in facilities at the University of Pennsylvania.
[25] Philadelphia Service Institute, "Philadelphia Service Institute Program," 1981, p. II-2.

that the consequences of shoplifting threaten a person's lifestyle, making shoplifting not worth the risk.

Education may be the key factor in reducing incidences of shoplifting. If, as surveys indicate, most shoplifters do not think about the consequences of their crime, it is likely that a large number of shoppers who do not steal are equally unaware of them. The "five-fingered discount" costs everyone money. If nothing else, the greed that leads many people to consider shoplifting at one time or another can also help them recognize that a problem exists.

Selected Bibliography

Books

Conner, Lawrence, *The Shoplifters are Coming*, Reports, Inc., 1980.
Edwards, Loren E., *Shoplifting and Shrinkage Protection for Stores*, C. C. Thomas, 1976.

Articles

Beck, Esther Ann and Sherwood C. McIntyre, "MMPI Patterns of Shoplifters Within a College Population," *Psychological Reports*, vol. 41, 1977.
Bellur, Venkatakrishna V., "Shoplifting: Can It Be Prevented?" *Journal of the Academy of Marketing Science*, spring 1981.
"The Difference Between a Systems Approach and a Methods Approach," *Security Management*, May 1981.
Gardner, Roberta A., "To Catch a Thief," *D & B Reports*, January-February 1980.
"How Shoplifting is Draining the Economy," *Business Week*, Oct. 15, 1979.
Nulty, Peter, "Sensormatic Collars the Shoplifter," *Fortune*, Feb. 25, 1980.
Percy, Susan, "Laying Down the Law on Shoplifting," *Atlanta Weekly*, Aug. 30, 1981.
"Pilfering Urges," *Time*, Nov. 17, 1980.
"Shoplifting Soars — and Merchants Strike Back," *U.S. News & World Report*, Dec. 3, 1979.

Reports and Studies

National Coalition to Prevent Shoplifting, "National Research Report: 1980 Summary"; "Program Guide," 1981.
Westinghouse Evaluation Institute, "National Evaluation Program — Phase I: Assessment of Shoplifting and Employee Theft Programs," 1979.

Cover by Staff Artist Robert Redding

JUVENILE JUSTICE

by

Marc Leepson

July 27
1 9 7 9

Editor's Note: More than two million young persons were arrested for serious crimes last year, but there is evidence that juvenile crime is leveling off. In 1981, according to FBI statistics, persons under 18 accounted for 19.8 percent of those arrested for serious crimes, down from 24.0 percent in 1977. Juveniles accounted for 9.6 percent of the murders, 14.8 percent of the rapes, 28.6 percent of the robberies and 42.6 percent of the burglaries committed in this country in 1981.

JUVENILE JUSTICE

HOW to deal with juveniles who commit crimes is a question that troubles, indeed perplexes, society. The American system of juvenile justice veers between punishment and rehabilitation, administering a little of both. It is hardly surprising, therefore, that juvenile justice is under fire today on two counts: for being too lenient with youngsters who commit violent crimes, and for being too harsh with those who commit only minor offenses. These separate stands of criticism have led to two divergent trends.

The first, a movement to punish kids more severely for serious crimes, arises in reaction to the large number of serious crimes they committed. In 1977, the last year for which complete statistics are available, persons under 18 accounted for nearly 10 percent of the murders, 17 percent of the rapes, 32 percent of the robberies and 52 percent of the burglaries committed in this country, according to the Federal Bureau of Investigation *(see table, p. 123).*

On the other hand, since the early 1970s the federal government and most of the states have begun to remove from penal institutions youngsters under 18 who were arrested for minor offenses or for offenses not considered criminal if committed by adults. Known as status offenses, because they apply only to persons with the legal status of minors, they include such things as running away from home, truancy and being unmanageable.

According to the U.S. Law Enforcement Assistance Administration (LEAA), between 200,000 and 500,000 children are taken into custody each year as status offenders. Some of their offenses are such things as sexual promiscuity, using vile, obscene or vulgar language in a public place, associating with immoral persons, sleeping in the streets, frequenting places where alcoholic beverages are sold, and refusing to obey authorities.

"The problem is not that juvenile courts are too lenient," Charles Silberman wrote in his much-praised book *Criminal Violence, Criminal Justice,* "but that they are too lenient toward the wrong people." In their desire to help troubled youngsters, he wrote, juvenile court judges "spend the bulk of their time on juveniles charged with offenses that would not be crimes

at all if committed by adults. . . . These 'status offenses' . . .
account for at least half, and perhaps as much as two-thirds of
juvenile court time. As a result, little time or energy is left to
deal with those juveniles who commit serious crimes."[1]

"The message is clear," Sen. Edward M. Kennedy, D-Mass.,
told the International Association of Chiefs of Police convention
in New York City last Oct. 8, "if juveniles want to get locked up
they should skip school, run away from home or be deemed 'a
problem.' If they want to avoid jail, they are better off committing a robbery or burglary. The two-track system of separate
adult and juvenile courts often makes a mockery of our criminal
justice system and undermines respect for the law. . . ."

Many Americans, especially those in large cities, have been
forced to alter their daily lives in fear of crime. "There is . . .
probably no aspect of urban society that strikes more terror in
city residents than the prospect of being confronted by" a
juvenile intent on committing a crime, Nicholas Pileggi wrote.
"The multimillion-dollar juvenile justice system, set up specially to deal with this problem has actually made the situation
worse."[2]

Public pressure to deal more harshly with juveniles accused of
crimes of violence has influenced most of the states to change
their laws in recent years to allow prison sentences for youngsters convicted of felonies. Forty-eight states (all but Nebraska
and Vermont) allow juveniles accused of serious crimes to be
tried in criminal courts, although circumstances vary from state
to state.

Criminal Trials for New York's Teenagers

The New York legislature passed a law last fall that observers
say is the most stringent juvenile crime statute on record. It
requires all 13-year-olds charged with murder and all 14- and 15-
year-olds accused of any serious crime to be tried in a criminal
court. New York already had a law treating those 16 and older as
adults if accused of a major crime. Under the new law, a juvenile
may face a maximum sentence of life in prison if convicted.
"Family courts just aren't relating to reality," Bronx County
District Attorney Mario Merola said of the new law and the
reasons it went into effect. "This law is absolutely necessary
because it addresses one of the most important problems in
criminal justice today."[3]

Criticism of the New York law centers on the belief that it
does little to reduce juvenile crime. Moreover, some persons
have voiced fears that children accused of relatively minor

[1] Charles E. Silberman, *Criminal Violence, Criminal Justice* (1978), p. 311.
[2] Writing in *New York* magazine, June 13, 1977, p. 36.
[3] Quoted in *Newsweek*, April 16, 1979, p. 54.

crimes will be treated and housed with those accused of rape and murder, unfairly branding the minor offender as a criminal. *The New York Times* characterized the law as "hastily conceived and needlessly harsh" in an editorial on May 29. The newspaper said that the law has not helped reduce juvenile crime rates and has served only to clog the state's already overcrowded criminal courts with juvenile cases. About two-thirds of the juvenile cases heard this year in New York's criminal courts were either dismissed or sent to Family (juvenile) Court, the *Times* said, adding that adolescents awaiting criminal trials were being jailed with adults.

—Department of Justice
photo by J. Wayne Higgs

John Rector, a Justice Department special counsel who formerly headed the Office of Juvenile Justice and Delinquency Prevention in the LEAA, wrote recently summarizing the federal government's position on the issue. "Some youthful offenders must be removed from their homes, but detention and incarceration should be reserved for those who commit serious, usually violent, offenses. Such custody should be provided in small community-based settings."[4]

Washington State's Point Plan for Offenders

In contrast to the New York law, the state of Washington last year set in motion a series of changes in its juvenile justice system that deal principally with the problem of administering justice to status offenders. Under the law, which went into effect July 1, 1978, status offenders and most minor offenders are dealt with outside the jurisdiction of the state criminal justice system. Community agencies now are charged with deciding on penalties for juvenile status offenders as well as with providing them with social rehabilitative services. But juveniles convicted of serious offenses and chronic offenders are sent to institutions.

Offenders under 18 are assigned a certain number of points, depending on their age and previous record. If a juvenile accumulates more than 110 points, he or she is given over to state judicial authorities for a fixed period of time and cannot be paroled. Those with fewer points may have to make restitution

---

[4] Writing in *IES Prison Law Monitor*, June 1979, p. 13.

to victims, pay fines or do community service work in hospitals or for local government agencies. If a juvenile fails to do these things, he or she is sent to a juvenile detention center for up to 30 days.

The law also accords children new rights, including the right of runaways to refuse to return home. The state is in the process of certifying a network of eight regional "crisis residential centers," where state-paid counselors will work to try to solve the problems of chronic runaways and other children. The eight regional centers will be supplemented by 30 family crisis residential centers, which will be less heavily staffed.

If the problems between parent and child cannot be worked out within three days, the family will be sent to court. But the juvenile court judges cannot send an unwilling child home. The alternatives are institutionalization, therapy or counseling. The new legal rights of children under Washington's 1978 law and supplemental changes in legislation passed this year "come as close as that of any other state to constituting a 'bill of rights' for children," writes Michael S. Serrill, executive editor of *Corrections* and *Police* magazines. "Children are no longer the chattels of their parents."[5]

In general, Washington's juvenile justice officials are pleased with the changes. "We're quite well satisfied with what we've been able to do keeping status offenders out of the criminal justice system," Denzel Scott, program manager for crisis intervention of the state's Department of Social and Health Services, said recently.[6] Before the law went into effect, about one-third of the status offenders were sent to foster homes. In the last year, the ratio was halved to one-sixth. "That is a substantial reduction," Scott said. "A lot of it has to do with the impact of the crisis intervention program for families in conflict." Warren Netherland, director of the Division of Juvenile Rehabilitation, told Editorial Research Reports that the new system was working out "reasonably well." "We still have some concerns, including the fact that lots of judges don't like the limitation [on sentences]. I don't think anybody knows what the effects of the new programs will be. It's far too early to make any conclusions."

Use of Community Programs in Massachusetts

The nationwide movement to get status offenders out of juvenile homes and state training schools (what used to be known as reform schools) began in the late 1960s. Massachusetts was the trend-setter in the movement. Its "deinstitutionalization" of all but the most violent juvenile offenders began in 1969 when

[5] Writing in *Saturday Review*, June 23, 1979, p. 22.
[6] Telephone interview, July 17, 1979.

U.S. Arrests, 1977

Offense charged	All ages	Under 18	Per-cent
Criminal homicide:			
(a) Murder and non-negligent manslaughter	17,163	1,670	9.7
(b) Manslaughter by negligence	2,933	327	11.1
Forcible rape	25,800	4,257	16.5
Robbery	122,514	39,259	32.0
Aggravated assault	221,329	36,182	16.3
Burglary	454,193	233,904	51.5
Larceny-theft	1,006,915	431,747	42.9
Motor vehicle theft	135,196	71,648	53.0
Other assaults	399,854	76,386	19.1
Arson	16,525	8,235	49.8
Forgery and counterfeiting	67,984	8,722	12.8
Fraud	216,672	22,377	10.3
Embezzlement	6,607	782	11.8
Stolen property: buying, receiving, possessing	104,401	34,307	32.9
Vandalism	196,724	118,563	60.3
Weapons; carrying, possessing, etc.	136,214	21,852	16.0
Prostitution and commercialized vice	77,115	3,315	4.3
Sex offenses (except forcible rape and prostitution)	60,959	11,197	18.4
Drug abuse violations	569,293	132,316	23.2
Gambling	52,520	2,204	4.2
Offenses against family and children	53,385	3,159	5.9
Driving under the influence	1,104,132	24,495	2.2
Liquor laws	321,573	119,913	37.3
Drunkenness	1,208,525	49,844	4.1
Disorderly conduct	624,736	121,272	19.4
Vagrancy	44,172	5,595	12.7
All other offenses (except traffic)	1,487,133	309,023	20.8
Suspicion	23,308	6,182	26.5
Curfew and loitering law violations	86,013	86,013	100.0
Runaways	185,447	185,447	100.0
Total	**9,029,335**	**2,170,193**	**24.0**

Source: Federal Bureau of Investigation

Labeling Juvenile Offenders

A person under age 18 who violates any provision of the juvenile code, either criminal or non-criminal, is labeled a "delinquent" in most states. However, some states reserve that term only for minors found guilty of a criminal offense.

Those under 18 who are arrested for minor offenses or for things which would not be considered crimes if committed by adults, are commonly known as status offenders because of their status as minors. But some states have other labels for these persons, including Persons in Need of Supervision (PINS), Minors in Need of Supervision (MINS), Children in Need of Supervision (CHINS), or Wayward, Unruly, Ungovernable, Incorrigible, Miscreant or Beyond Control Children.

Jerome Miller was appointed director of the state's Department of Youth Services.

By 1972, thousands of juvenile offenders had been transferred back to their homes or into small, community-based programs. "Today, on any day, less than 100 juveniles are being held in secure facilities in the state," said Miller, who now is president of the National Center on Institutions and Alternatives in Washington, D.C. "Even those tend to be in small units of 10-12 kids per unit. Between 60 and 80 percent of the state's incarcerated juveniles returned to jail under the old system," Miller said. Brutality was common in the facilities, and it cost the state some $10,000 a year to house each child. Most of the money went toward maintaining the facilities, some of which were in bad disrepair.

"Miller's reform sparked a national debate that has barely subsided," *Corrections* magazine commented last year. "The closing of large secure facilities and the almost total reliance on such programs as home treatment, foster care and group homes shocked legislators, judges, and law enforcement officials."[7] A recent study by Harvard University sociologists Lloyd Ohlin, Robert Coates and Alden Miller found no statewide drop in recidivism with the new system, although there were lower rates in certain regions of the state.

Miller, who left the Massachusetts post in 1973, continues to speak out against the jailing of juvenile offenders. "For what it costs to institutionalize kids you can pay one person a salary and give them a kid," he said recently in an interview. "In some states you can hire two or three people for each juvenile. You pay them a full salary, train them and you've got individual care that is as close as we can get to family care — the only viable treatment in our society."

---

[7] *Corrections*, September 1978, p. 13.

"Juvenile institutions are brutal crime factories," Miller contends. "What we have now in most states is as if you asked a group from organized crime to design a system to turn out more street criminals."

Miller said juveniles convicted of violent crimes should be kept "off the street for quite a while, in small, secure units where they can receive very individualized services. If you set such a system up today, there would only be about 250 kids under 18 locked up in the state of New York."

Development of the U.S. System

THE BASIC question in the history of treatment of juveniles in the United States has been whether to punish juvenile offenders like adults or to treat them separately with a view toward their rehabilitation. Until the Industrial Revolution and even beyond that, children past infancy were regarded as little adults. The concept of adolescence was unknown. In matters of criminal justice, children tended to be treated the same as adults. English common law pardoned children under age seven for all acts, but those eight to 14 were held responsible for their conduct if they were judged to be sufficiently intelligent to understand the nature of their behavior and if they could distinguish right from wrong. Over age 14, they were considered to be adults.

This thinking began to change only in the last century. The concept of juvenile delinquency — as opposed to a general concept of crime to be dealt with irrespective of age — emerged when interest in deterring and punishing young offenders gradually shifted to a concern for reforming and rehabilitating them. At first, voluntary groups alone carried out the task of rehabilitating delinquents. The first Ragged Schools for destitute or abandoned children were set up in England in 1818.

In the United States, the "child-saving movement" led to the establishment of training schools designed to keep minors out of jail. The first such institution was the House of Refuge, founded in New York City in 1825 by the Society for the Reformation of Juvenile Delinquents. The children, some of whom were street urchins, lived in a grim building that had been a troop barracks. The first publicly supported school for delinquents was established in 1847 in Massachusetts.

The philosophy behind the American reform schools underwent little change for decades. Their primary purpose was to guard delinquents from the influences that had led them astray, to instill in them a respect for authority and to teach them a trade. The schools stressed rigid discipline, religious instruction and "busy work." Reformers promoted the idea during the 1850s that children and youths could be rehabilitated more easily if placed in a rural setting. It was thought that cities bred delinquency and that country living put children in a healthier frame of mind.

Concept of Juvenile Delinquency and Reform

The brutality of incarcerating children with adult criminals led gradually to efforts to separate the two groups. In 1861, the mayor of Chicago appointed a commissioner to hear and rule on minor charges against boys 6 to 17 years old, and to place them on probation or in a reformatory if found guilty. An 1870 Massachusetts law required that children's cases in Suffolk County (Boston) be heard separately from adult cases, and it authorized a representative of the state to investigate cases, attend trials and protect children's interests. The statute was extended throughout Massachusetts two years later. In 1877, separate dockets and court records were provided in juvenile cases. New York adopted similar provisions in 1892, as did Rhode Island in 1898.

It was in Illinois, however, where the first statewide court for children was established. The Juvenile Court Act of 1899 included most of the features that have since come to distinguish the juvenile court system. The law formally codified the concept of *parens patriae*[8] and gave the state discretionary power over the welfare of children. The court, in effect, became a substitute parent. Other states quickly enacted similar laws — Wisconsin and New York in 1901, Ohio and Maryland in 1902 and Colorado in 1903. Within a dozen years, 22 states had followed the Illinois ˉˉample and by 1925 special juvenile courts existed in 46 states.

The object of the new juvenile court system was not to punish or apportion guilt, but to save children from the corrupt influence of urban life and steer them on the road to recovery by giving them care, treatment, discipline and responsible supervision. The system was very different from the criminal justice system. A juvenile court judge sat at a desk or table instead of behind a bench. In an informal atmosphere, the judge acted fatherly and sympathetic while still appearing authoritative.

A new vocabulary symbolized the new philosophy that emphasized socio-psychological services rather than punishment. A child was not arrested, but "taken into custody," "detained," or

---

[8] Literally, "father of the country," the Latin phrase conveys the legal concept of a state official paternally taking charge of the interest of persons without parents or guardians or of those incapable of conducting their affairs. See "Juvenile Offenders," *E.R.R.*, 1970 Vol. I, pp. 99-118.

"referred" to a juvenile court. The child was not sentenced but assigned to a "dispositional alternative" such as a state "training school." He or she was not imprisoned in a penal institution, but "remanded" to a reformatory for rehabilitation and supervision.

The individual's background was more important than the facts of a given case. Because it was important that the child be protected from the ordeal of criminal court, there was to be no adversary proceeding in the new juvenile court system. Lawyers were seldom present in court and many juvenile judges were not lawyers. Juvenile courts were largely administered by social workers and others without legal training.

Many observers concluded that the new juvenile court system worked splendidly. Reformers such as Julia Lathrop, Jane Addams, and Edith and Grace Abbott were among those who praised the system in its early years. Jane Addams, a founding member of the pioneering children's court in Chicago and proprietor of that city's Hull House, one of the first social settlements in the United States, said, "there was almost a change in mores when the juvenile court was established."[9]

Judge Julian Mack wrote in the *Harvard Law Review* in 1909: "The problem for determination by the judge is not, Has this boy or girl committed a specific wrong, but What is he, How has he become what he is, and what had best be done in his interest and in the interest of the state to save him from a downward career." The goal of the juvenile court, he added, is "not so much to punish as to reform, not to degrade but to uplift, not to crush but to develop, not to make him a criminal but a worthy citizen."

Supreme Court Decisions Protecting Youths

In spite of the lofty goals of and the general praise for the juvenile justice system, one essential component was missing — constitutional due process of law. Juveniles suspected of violating the law were not given written notice of the charges against them, did not have the right to legal counsel or the privilege to refuse to testify, nor did they have the right to confront and cross-examine witnesses or challenge evidence. But the U.S. Supreme Court, handing down its first major decision in a case involving the juvenile justice system, ruled in 1967 that due process must be provided in juvenile cases. In the landmark case, *In Re Gault* (387 U.S. 1), the court held that children brought before a juvenile court were entitled to the same procedural protections afforded by the Bill of Rights to adults in the criminal justice system. "Under our Constitution," the court

[9] Quoted in Silberman, *op. cit.*, p. 310.

said in its written decision, "the condition of being a boy does not justify a kangaroo court."

Two subsequent Supreme Court decisions broadened the juvenile's constitutional rights. The court held March 31, 1970, *In the Matter of Samuel Winship* (397 U.S. 358) that juveniles charged with a crime, like adults, are constitutionally entitled to proof beyond a reasonable doubt. The court ruled unconstitutional a New York law under which 12-year-old Samuel Winship was tried and convicted in 1967 in New York Family Court for stealing $112 from a pocketbook. That law provided that the standard of proof for guilt in juvenile proceedings could fall short of the "beyond a reasonable doubt" standard. Winship's lawyers successfully argued that the state law was unconstitutional.

The Supreme Court agreed with the dissenting opinion of a New York Court of Appeals judge, which stated: "Where a 12-year-old child is charged with an act of stealing which renders him liable to confinement for as long as six years, then as a matter of due process ... the case against him must be proved beyond a reasonable doubt."

On June 21, 1971, in *McKeiver v. Pennsylvania* (403 U.S. 528), the court ruled in the case of a 16-year-old Pennsylvania boy, Joseph McKeiver, who requested a jury trial after being charged with robbery, larceny and receiving stolen goods. The court said that a jury is not needed for accurate fact-finding, and therefore a jury trial is not constitutionally required in a juvenile case. "Compelling a jury trial might remake the proceedings into a fully adversary process and effectively end the idealistic prospect of an intimate, informal, protective proceeding," Justice Harry A. Blackmun said on behalf of the Supreme Court. A lawyer writing four years later in *Trial* magazine said the decision constituted "a conscious process of balancing society's interest in protecting individual rights with the preservation of the basic element unique to juvenile courts, that of intimate informal hearings."[10]

The Federal Juvenile Justice Act of 1974

Congress in 1974 enacted the Juvenile Justice and Delinquency Act to expand and coordinate federal programs for the prevention and correction of juvenile delinquency and to reform the states' juvenile justice systems. The law signaled the lawmakers' intention to stress the rehabilitative aspect of juvenile justice. It set up within the Justice Department's Law Enforcement Assistance Administration (LEAA) an Office of Juvenile Justice and Delinquency Prevention to administer most of the

---

[10] Jean B. Chalmers, *Trial,* July-August 1975, p. 65. *Trial* is published by the Association of Trial Lawyers of America.

Increase in Juvenile Arrests

Offense charged	Change 1968-77
Criminal homicide:	
(a) Murder and nonnegligent manslaughter	+ 38.1%
(b) Manslaughter by negligence	+ 15.1
Forcible rape	+ 32.9
Robbery	+ 50.1
Aggravated assault	+ 76.6
Burglary	+ 28.1
Larceny-theft	+ 37.2
Motor vehicle theft	− 24.0
Other assaults	+ 56.5
Arson	+ 10.7
Forgery and counterfeiting	+ 62.5
Fraud	+ 97.2
Embezzlement	+176.3
Stolen property; buying, receiving, possessing	+127.2
Vandalism	+ 12.9
Weapons; carrying, possessing, etc.	+ 26.9
Prostitution and commercialized vice	+241.8
Sex offenses (except forcible rape and prostitution)	− 18.3
Drug abuse violations	+130.1
Gambling	− 5.4
Offenses against family and children	+264.8
Driving under the influence	+371.2
Liquor laws	+ 33.4
Drunkenness	− 3.0
Disorderly conduct	− 10.8
Vagrancy	− 55.8
All other offenses (except traffic)	+ 9.4
Suspicion (not included in totals)	− 79.8
Curfew and loitering law violations	− 38.1
Runaways	− 6.0
Total	+ 17.8

Source: Federal Bureau of Investigation

federal programs for prevention and treatment of juvenile delinquency. Some of these programs had previously been administered by other offices in LEAA and by the Department of Health, Education and Welfare.

The law provided federal grants for states to (1) improve their juvenile justice systems, with emphasis on the diversion of juveniles from criminal incarceration to a less severe form of supervision such as halfway houses, and (2) assist the states in providing shelter, counseling and medical services to truants,

129

uncontrollable and, especially, runaway children.[11] The law also established the National Advisory Committee for Juvenile Justice and Delinquency Prevention, a 21-member board appointed by the president to help coordinate improvements in the nation's juvenile justice systems. Seven of the committee's members must be under the age of 26 and all must have special knowledge about the prevention or treatment of juvenile delinquency.

Congress in 1977 extended the 1974 legislation for three more years and revised it modestly. The 1977 amendments provided for "special emphasis" programs in the areas of school violence and vandalism,[12] the protection of the rights of youths in the criminal justice system, and for assistance to state legislatures in drafting legislation to assure compliance with the mandates of the Juvenile Justice Act.

"The General Accounting Office has called the act the most promising and cost-effective federal crime prevention effort," said John Rector, former director of the Office of Juvenile Justice and Delinquency Prevention. Previously as head counsel of the Senate Subcommittee to Investigate Juvenile Delinquency, he was the chief architect of the 1974 legislation. ". . .Congress has called upon the states, localities, public and private agencies, and others, to reassess the rationale which has made institutionalization the favored alternative far too often," Rector added.[13]

U.S. Funding Pressure on States to Conform

Federal grants became the catalyst for bringing about change in several states that long had incarcerated youngsters. These included California, Georgia, Pennsylvania, Virginia, Washington, Wisconsin and West Virginia. All of them passed laws or changed administrative rules to prohibit the jailing of status offenders. The Office of Juvenile Justice, for example, held up grants to the California Youth Authority for two years because its schools and training programs enrolled youths ranging in age from 17 to 21. The federal law required, as a condition of funding, that youths under 18 be held separately.

Some $9.2 million was awarded to the various states through the grant program in fiscal year 1975, the first year in which the 1974 act took effect. The grants rose to a peak of $71.9 million in 1978 before dipping to $61.6 million in 1979 budget economizing. Six states — Nebraska, Nevada, Oklahoma, Wyoming, North Dakota and South Dakota — have refused to participate and thus have forfeited their federal grant money.

---

[11] For details, see Congressional Quarterly's 1974 *Almanac,* p. 278.

[12] For background, see "Violence in the Schools," *E.R.R.,* 1976 Vol. II, pp. 581-600.

[13] Quoted in *LEAA Newsletter,* October 1977, p. 5.

The Office of Juvenile Justice reported that as of mid-1979, 14 states — Connecticut, Delaware, Indiana, Iowa, Louisiana, Maine, Maryland, Massachusetts, Minnesota, New Jersey, Oklahoma, Pennsylvania, Washington and Wisconsin — set a 24-hour limit on the time a status offender may be held in secure detention facilities. Six other states — Arkansas, California, Florida, Illinois, Oregon and Virginia — have a 72-hour limit. Most of the states, the agency reported, prohibit the detention of youngsters in facilities with adults.

Proposals for Further Change

AT ITS 1979 midwinter meeting in Atlanta, the American Bar Association adopted a broad set of principles calling for sweeping changes in the entire juvenile justice system. The proposals were drawn up by an ABA commission headed by Irving Kaufman, chief judge of the U.S. Court of Appeals in New York, which had spent eight years studying the juvenile justice system. The bar association delegates approved 14 of the 17 sets of recommendations made by the committee, including a "due process" model law entitling juvenile defendants to all due process rights that adults have, such as open hearings and jury trials.

Observers say the most important recommendation is that judges sentence offenders to specific terms related to the severity of the crime, the age of the offender and the juvenile's criminal record. In most states, the amount of time juveniles spend in correctional facilities is likely to be determined by the findings of social workers or probation officers. The ABA recommendations also set standards for police handling of juveniles and enumerated offenders' rights in correctional institutions.

It is expected that the state legislatures will take the ABA recommendations into account when they consider changes in their juvenile justice systems. One provision of the ABA recommendations, that status offenders be removed from the criminal justice system, was not considered at the February meeting. It was dropped from the agenda because of opposition from juvenile court judges and others, but Judge Kaufman said the proposal will be resubmitted next year. The ABA's refusal to support the proposal "must be regarded as a a major setback" in juvenile justice reform, said Leonard Troppin, vice president of the National Council on Crime and Delinquency.[14]

John Rector wrote recently that the U.S. juvenile justice

---

[14] Quoted in *The Christian Science Monitor*, Feb. 14, 1979.

system needs "an uncompromising departure from the current practice of institutional overkill."[15] Senator Kennedy, while advocating "significant punishment" for juveniles who commit violent crimes, told the International Association of Chiefs of Police last year that this country needs to "take the juvenile courts out of the business of punishing status offenders or jailing the 'problem child.' " Charles Silberman, who investigated the treatment of juvenile offenders across the country, wrote last year that "there can be no excuse for holding status offenders or youngsters accused of minor offenses in adult jails, or in secure detention centers."[16]

Silberman suggested that juvenile court judges "need an array of non-custodial punishments — ways of responding to delinquent or criminal behavior that make it clear that sanctions *are* [his emphasis] being imposed, without incarcerating or otherwise damaging the youngsters in the process." The 1974 Juvenile Justice Act and its 1977 amendments are intended primarily to do just that — to foster the development of programs that divert more juveniles from the juvenile justice process and to help states, localities and public agencies set up alternatives to detention and correctional facilities.

Federal Grants to Improve Youth Services

The government has awarded grants to various private, state and local agencies across the country under the 1974 law. Last year, for example, the Office of Juvenile Justice and Delinquency Prevention funded a two-year program in Memphis, Tenn., called the Memphis Diversion Project. The project's $776,000 federal grant is aimed at (1) preventing children from being declared delinquent and (2) sending them to counseling agencies rather than to detention facilities. The Memphis Board of Education's Division of Special Education and three other agencies are participating in the project. These groups provide family and individual counseling and help the young people obtain job training and outpatient drug and alcohol counseling.

Initial results are encouraging. Of the first 385 juveniles selected for the project's services, only 10 percent had been rearrested, the *LEAA Newsletter* reported in February. This compares to a recidivism rate of 35 percent of juvenile offenders not in the program. "Children who violate the law and who are considered a threat to the community need to be reached," said the project's director, Michael Whitaker. "These youngsters are those who need to be diverted from the system in a meaningful way. We can't simply chalk them off as juvenile delinquents and forget about them."[17]

---

[15] Writing in *IES Prison Law Monitor, op. cit.*, p. 13.
[16] Silberman, *op. cit.*, p. 323.
[17] Quoted in *LEAA Newsletter*, February 1978, p. 7.

Scared Straight?

The movie "Scared Straight" won the Academy Award for best feature-length documentary of 1978, and was subsequently shown to a nationwide television audience. It gives a vivid, close-up picture of the Juvenile Awareness Project Help run by the Lifers Group of inmates at the maximum security Rahway State Prison in New Jersey. Hardened convicts shout obscenities and tell the straight story about prison life to 17 juveniles who have had brushes with the law. Narrator Peter Falk concludes the show by saying that three months after the filming only one of the teenagers had gotten into trouble, and that of the 10,000 juveniles taken through the program since it began in 1976, 90 percent had not been arrested again.

The 90 percent figure comes from a Lifers Group survey undertaken with the help of Judge George Nicola, Juvenile and Domestic Relations Court Judge in Middlesex, N.J., one of the program's ardent supporters. Agencies that sent juveniles through the program were asked how they were faring. Of the agencies that responded, nearly all said that in general the kids were doing well.

James O. Finckenauer, associate professor at the Rutgers University School of Criminal Justice, offers a different finding, however. He began an investigation of the program's results in December 1977. Finckenauer reported in November 1978 that of a group of juveniles who had gone through the program, he found that 58.7 percent did not get into trouble afterward. Of a comparable group of youths who did not attend the program, 88.6 percent did not repeat as offenders. "It's simplistic to think this is the answer," Finckenauer told *Youth Alternatives* magazine.* "Delinquency just doesn't lend itself to simple solutions."

*May 1979 issue

Grants from the Office of Juvenile Justice also have been made to youth advocacy groups, whose job is to assure that proper services are being provided the young people and their families who are involved in the juvenile justice system.[18] One such organization, the National Juvenile Law Center in St. Louis, Mo., received an 18-month grant Oct. 1, 1978, to establish and conduct the Youth Legal Assistance Project in Iowa, Kentucky, Maryland, New Jersey, Pennsylvania and Tennessee. The aim is to help youth advocacy groups in those states plan and push for legislative programs requiring, among other things,

[18] See *Nations Cities Weekly*, Dec. 11, 1978.

Youth Population

The long-term future of juvenile crime could hinge on demographics — specifically on an expected shrinkage and then another expansion in the size of the nation's youth population. According to projections by the U.S. Census Bureau, today's unusually large youth population is entering a period of decline. Those aged 14 through 24 made up 20.8 percent of the U.S. population in 1975 but are expected to form only 15 to 16 percent in 1990. The drop in actual numbers of 14-24 years old, however, may be as little as 3.9 million or as great as 5.4 million, depending on which of three sets of Census Bureau assumptions about future fertility rates one chooses to accept. Moreover, by 1990, the youth population will be on the increase again, according to two of the calculations.

the separation of juveniles from incarcerated adults. With a similar aim, the Youth Law Center in San Francisco received a grant in September 1978 to provide legal services to advocacy organizations in Colorado, New Mexico, North Carolina, Oregon, Utah and Washington.[19]

The National Youth Work Alliance has received $1.2 million in federal grants primarily to train youth workers and assist them in advocacy efforts aimed at setting up community-based correctional facilities in Iowa, Michigan, New Hampshire, North Carolina, Ohio, Oklahoma, Oregon, Washington and Wisconsin. Another $1.2 million grant went to the National Center on Institution Alternatives, a private non-profit organization with headquarters in Washington, D.C., for a project called Juvenile Alternative Correctional Treatment Systems. The project will recommend changes within the juvenile corrections systems in Maryland, New York City, Puerto Rico and Utah. The main goal is to create and implement a range of alternative programs for delinquent youths and to reduce the juvenile correctional institutions' populations by 50 percent in those jurisdictions.

View That Problem is Beyond Scope of Law

Not everyone agrees that deinstitutionalization is the principal answer for the nation's juvenile justice problems. Robert Wagner, superintendent of the Rhode Island Training School for Boys and Girls, wrote last year that the problem "is not that of institutions alone, although they bear the brunt of criticism and play the scapegoat role. The roots lie deeper. They are in the administration, at both higher and lower echelons." Wagner said that the "real question . . . is not the building of alternatives, but rather how to avoid erecting the same system with

---

[19] See *IES Prison Law Monitor*, June 1979, p. 19.

Change in Britain

In Britain, Prime Minister Margaret Thatcher's new Tory government has begun moving that nation toward conservatism. But the government's recently announced plan for fighting juvenile crime is akin to the most innovative American program, in Massachusetts *(see p. 122)*, in which juveniles convicted of all but the most violent crimes are kept out of secure detention facilities.

The Tory government's new plan, which was put forth early in July, does include tough new penalties for juveniles over 16 who are convicted of the crime of "mindless adventure," which includes vandalism and hooliganism at football (soccer) games. But the main changes call for treating most juvenile offenders in community-based programs rather than in institutions. The move was based partly on the high cost of Britain's juvenile justice detention centers, where the state spends over $10,000 a year on each incarcerated youth.

A government commission that studied the Massachusetts juvenile justice system recently recommended the changes. "The Massachusetts model is the going thing now in Europe," said Jerome Miller, who instituted the Massachusetts plan. In addition to Britain, "Norway is talking about it and so is West Germany."

new names. The creation of smaller institutions, group homes, foster care, diversionary programs, and the like serve as a mere palliative treatment of the overall juvenile justice system if, in fact, we build just another system."[20]

Wagner suggested that the juvenile correction system needs to attract dedicated workers and that communities must show enough concern to become involved with juveniles who are in trouble. Wagner agrees with most observers of the criminal justice system in his belief that the nation's juvenile crime problem cannot be solved solely by reforming the juvenile justice system. There are immense social problems associated with juvenile crime. "While it may not be the courts' proper role to address the history of poverty, discrimination, abuse and deprivation that most defendants carry with them to the courtroom," Michael S. Serrill wrote, "it is certainly someone's responsibility."[21] Unless and until those problems are addressed, juvenile crime will remain one of this nation's vexing problems.

---

[20] Writing in *Criminology*, February 1978, p. 439.
[21] Serrill, *op. cit.*, p. 24.

Selected Bibliography

Books

Coates, Robert B., et al., *Diversity in a Youth Correctional System: Handling Delinquents in Massachusetts*, Ballinger, 1978.

Flicker, Barbara D., *Standards for Juvenile Justice: A Summary and Analysis*, Ballinger, 1977.

Kahn, Alfred, *A Court for Children*, Columbia University Press, 1953.

Klein, Malcolm W., ed., *The Juvenile Justice System*, Sage Publications, 1976.

Rosenheim, Margaret K., ed., *Pursuing Justice for the Child*, University of Chicago Press, 1976.

Schlossman, Steven L., *Love and the American Delinquent: The Theory and Practice of "Progressive" Juvenile Justice, 1825-1920*, University of Chicago Press, 1977.

Silberman, Charles E., *Criminal Violence, Criminal Justice*, Random House, 1978.

Van den Haag, Ernest, *Punishing Criminals: Concerning a Very Old and Painful Question*, Basic Books, 1975.

Articles

Boland, Barbara and James Q. Wilson, "Age, Crime and Punishment," *Public Interest*, spring 1978.

"Children in Jail," *The Progressive*, April 1979.

Chalmers, Jean B., "Rejuvenating Juvenile Courts," *Trial Magazine*, July-August 1975.

Corrections, selected issues.

Harris, Lis, "Persons in Need of Supervision," *The New Yorker*, Aug. 14, 1978.

Pileggi, Nicholas, "How Fifteen-Year-Olds Get Away with Murder," *New York*, June 13, 1977.

Rector, John "Juvenile Justice: A Congressional Priority," *Judicature*, June-July 1977.

Serrill, Michael S., "The Search for Juvenile Justice," *Saturday Review*, June 23, 1979.

Wagner, Robert, "The System Listens But Does Not Hear," *Criminology*, February 1978.

Reports and Studies

Editorial Research Reports, "Violence in the Schools," 1976 Vol. II, p. 583; "Juvenile Offenders," 1970 Vol. I, p. 99; "Reform of Delinquents," 1957 Vol. II, p. 525.

Knitzer, Jane and Mary Lee Allen, "Children Without Homes: An Examination of Public Responsibility to Children in Out of Home Placement," Children's Defense Fund, November 1978.

President's Commission on Law Enforcement and Administration of Justice, "Juvenile Delinquency and Youth Crime," 1967.

U.S. Department of Justice, Federal Bureau of Investigation, "Uniform Crime Reports for the United States," Oct. 18, 1978.

COLLEGE
ADMISSIONS

by

John Kotler

Apr. 11
1 9 8 0

Editor's Note: Applications for freshman admissions at public and private four-year colleges were down 1.6 percent at the end of July 1982 compared with a year earlier, *The Chronicle of Higher Education* reported July 28, 1982. In contrast, enrollment at public two-year colleges was expected to increase 4 percent.

According to the National Center for Educational Statistics, tuition costs at public colleges rose an average of 66 percent from 1974-75 to 1981-82; private college tuition went up 89 percent. President Reagan has sought sharp cuts in the two largest student aid programs: the Pell Grants (named after Sen. Claiborne Pell, D-R.I) and the guaranteed student loan program. Although Congress did not go as far as the president wanted, it did make cutbacks in the two programs *(see box, p. 16)*.

SAT scores have remained fairly stable in recent years *(see p. 144)*. The average score on the verbal section of the test was 427 in 1979-80 and 424 in 1980-81. The average score on the math section was 466 both years.

COLLEGE ADMISSIONS

EVERY year about this time, millions of high school seniors exhibit similar symptoms — bouts of anxiety, irritability and a tendency to wait by the mail box. The object of all these concerns is the letter telling them whether they will be admitted or rejected by the college of their choice. For the most part, the letters arrive by mid-April. The vast majority of college candidates probably have less to worry about than they realize. The number of students in the traditional undergraduate age bracket has declined in recent years *(see p. 151)* and some schools already have fewer applicants than they need to fill their classrooms. As a result, many colleges are aggressively recruiting new students.[1]

Nearly four out of five freshman applicants at public and private four-year colleges now are being accepted, according to a survey published last fall by the American Association of Collegiate Registrars and Admissions Officers (AACRAO) and the College Board, a non-profit education association. Private four-year schools, which usually are thought of as having the toughest entrance requirements, accept more than 77 percent of those who apply. The comparable figures for public two-year colleges and private two-year colleges are 91 percent and 86 percent respectively *(see box, p. 141)*.

"The public perception that most colleges accept only a small percentage of persons who apply is simply not true," said James E. Nelson, the College Board's vice president for program research and planning. "The problem may be that the public mostly hears about only a few select, prestigious colleges. In fact, the vast majority of colleges . . . are not that hard to get into."

The findings of the College Board-AACRAO survey probably do little to allay the concerns of those who have applied to one of the nation's highly selective universities. Last year Harvard accepted only 2,249 of 13,089 applicants for the freshman class, a rate of 18 percent, followed by 21 percent at Princeton and 24

---

[1] See "College Recruiting," *E.R.R.*, 1974 Vol. II, pp. 661-680.

[2] The results of "The College Board-AACRAO Survey of Undergraduate Admissions Policies, Practices and Procedures" were presented at the College Board's 1979 annual meeting, held Oct. 30 in New Orleans.

percent at Yale.[3] Among the factors that determine who is accepted at the Ivy League and other prestigious schools are scores on college entrance examinations such as the Scholastic Aptitude Test (SAT) prepared for the College Board by the Educational Testing Service. About 1.5 million SATs were administered last year. Nearly a million students took the comparable American College Testing Program (ACT) exam.

Nearly 60 percent of the public four-year colleges and 54 percent of the private four-year schools responding to the College Board-AACRAO survey said that scores on standardized tests were a "very important factor" in admissions decisions. However, more than 27 percent of the public four-year colleges and nearly 40 percent of the private four-year colleges reported that test scores were either "one of several factors" considered or were "a minor factor." About 16 percent of the college officials surveyed said that SAT and ACT scores were less important today in making admissions decisions than in 1970. Although 40 percent of the institutions reported having a minimum grade point average below which applicants generally were not considered eligible for admission, less than 30 percent indicated having similar "minimum standards" for SAT scores.

Debate Over Use of Entrance Examinations

Using test scores as admissions criteria can present problems, as major testing organizations readily admit. The College Board issued guidelines in 1977 warning that test scores are "approximate rather than exact" measures of academic potential. "Test scores, like all types of measurements, physical as well as psychological, are not perfectly precise and should not be treated as though they were," the guidelines stated. The following year the board issued another warning to college admissions officers. "Test scores should not be the sole factor in determining the admission of an applicant . . . ," the board cautioned. "In most instances a student's high school record is the best available predictor of academic success in college, and a combination of high school record and scores is almost always better than either one alone."[4]

Despite such warnings some people believe college entrance examinations still play too large a role in college admissions. Consumer activist Ralph Nader recently issued a report that was highly critical of standardized entrance examinations, especially the SAT and other tests provided by the Educational Testing Service. In the preface to the report, Nader called the SAT a "one-time, three-hour gamble which can determine a

---

[3] Figures reported by Gene I. Maeroff in *The New York Times*, April 4, 1980.
[4] The College Board, "Taking the SAT," 1978, p. 48.

Freshmen Applicants Accepted and Enrolled
By Type of College

	Public Two-Year	Public Four-Year	Private Four-Year	Private Two-Year
Freshmen Applicants Accepted for Admission	90.7%	78.6%	77.5%	86.2%
Freshmen Applicants Actually Enrolled	77.3	53.2	47.7	65.5
Accepted Freshmen Applicants Actually Enrolled	81.3	65.8	59.8	73.5

Source: The College Board and the American Association of Collegiate Registrars and Admissions Officers, 1979.

life's pathway."[5] The report said the SAT and other ETS examinations, such as the Law School Admissions Test (LSAT), are used to limit access to the most selective undergraduate and professional schools and, thus, to the upper strata of American society. It cited studies which indicate that test scores often break down along socio-economic lines with the children of wealthy, educated parents consistently receiving high scores, while children of poor families generally score lowest. One reason for this, the report stated, is that the SAT has built-in cultural biases that make it difficult for minority members to score as well as their white counterparts.

The College Board contends that the SAT and other standardized tests have helped minorities, not harmed them. George H. Hanford, president of the College Board, believes standardized tests have allowed colleges to identify talented minority students who might otherwise have been overlooked. Edward A. Wynne, editor of *Character,* a magazine that focuses on public and private policies which affect young people, made a similar point. "Before the tests, [admissions] decisions were more individualized, and [colleges] used more and softer information," he wrote recently. "As a result, the decision makers were more prone to apply time-saving criteria such as the reputation of the applicant's high school, or whether he had relatives as alumni."[6]

In a memo to College Board members in February, Hanford acknowledged that minority students generally score below other students on the SAT. But he said this reflects their poor educational backgrounds not a bias on the exam. "The test does not create the difference, it mirrors and reveals it," he wrote.

---

[5] Allan Nairn and Associates, "The Reign of ETS: The Ralph Nader Report on the Educational Testing Service," January 1980, pp. xii-xiii.

[6] Writing in *The Wall Street Journal,* Feb. 14, 1980.

Hanford also claimed minority students have had more success entering college during the past decade than many people realize. From 1970 to 1977, he said, college enrollment increased 5 percent for blacks and 6 percent for Hispanics while it remained fairly constant for white students.

Perhaps the most serious charge in the Nader report was that the SAT is not very useful in predicting college success. Pure chance, "a role of the dice," would tell as much about a student's chances for success in the first year of college in 88 percent of the cases, the report said. Hanford sharply disagreed. In his February memo he cited the results of a 13-year study of the 19 colleges in the Georgia state university system that indicated that SAT scores provide "a strong, incremental addition" to the validity of admissions predictions when used in conjunction with high school grades.[7]

Even if the tests are helpful in predicting academic achievement, it is generally conceded that they tell little about success in later life. Attributes like drive, ingenuity and interpersonal skills seem to play a greater role in long-term achievement than either grades or test scores. Nader, in his preface to the report on the ETS, called for "broader, more diverse approaches for assessing individual performance . . . a multi-cultural array of evaluations, which can tap the untapped or unique talents of diverse individuals."

Some colleges use entrance examinations as a tool to assess student weaknesses rather than as a selective device. This seems to be especially true of the ACT exam, which is used by many colleges in the South, West and Midwest. Bob Elliot of ACT's Iowa City office said the test is designed primarily to aid high school and college counselors help students choose career and study paths, although it is also used for predicting academic performance.[8] Some educators believe all college entrance exams will be utilized less for selecting students and more for guiding them in the coming years.

Recent Enactment of 'Truth-in-Testing' Laws

Criticism of standardized entrance examinations has resulted in passage of "truth-in-testing" laws in California and New York. A national truth-in-testing law is being considered in Congress, and similar measures are being pushed in a number of states. The law passed by the California legislature in 1978 re-

---

[7] The Georgia study found that the SAT alone provided a correlation of 0.49 (out of a perfect 1.0) with success in the freshman year, compared to a 0.54 correlation for high school grades. Used together, however, the two measures provided a correlation of 0.65.

[8] Interview, April 3, 1980.

quires testing companies to provide the public with sample tests similar to the actual exams administered in the state. In July 1979, the New York legislature approved a more stringent law. It requires companies to provide the questions and answers for actual tests to those who request them after the scores are released.[9] The law was backed by the Parent-Teacher Association (PTA), the National Education Association and the American Federation of Teachers (AFL-CIO).

The truth-in-testing bill introduced in Congress in July 1979 is now before the House Education and Labor Committee. The bill has a disclosure requirement similar to the New York law. In addition, it would require the makers of standardized tests to provide test takers with a "clear overview" of the examination prior to administering the tests and to publicize the results of studies concerning the validity and reliability of entrance examinations. Supporters have said they are reviewing the bill and may submit a somewhat different version in the next few months.

At a press conference on April 7, President George H. Hanford announced that the College Board was taking a number of steps to give students more information about the content of tests and provide them with procedures for challenging test scores. Every autumn the board will publish one version of the exam that was used during the preceding year, along with a statistical analysis of its characteristics. Students taking the SAT will have an opportunity to verify their scores personally by receiving their answer sheet, a scoring key and scoring information. The fee for this optional service will be refunded if any discrepancy is found.

Hanford coupled his announcement with criticism of truth-in-testing laws, which he said "imposed misguided operational requirements which threaten test quality." The board has asked Congress and the state legislatures not to enact any new disclosure laws until there has been time to evaluate the effects of the New York law.

Diane Ravitch of Columbia University's Teachers College, believes the New York law will "accomplish few, if any, of its intended purposes." Instead of making tests less culturally biased, she said, the law will make it more difficult and expensive for test companies to take the time they now do to screen out questions which are slanted against minorities. She also said the law will have little effect on admissions procedures since most college admissions officers already understand the weaknesses of

---

[9] The New York law went into effect Jan. 1, 1980. The first SAT covered by the law was administered March 22. The courts have granted medical schools in the state a delay in implementing the law for their entrance exams.

tests and treat them accordingly. Some highly selective colleges will establish their own entrance exams if they feel disclosure is making standardized tests less reliable, she concluded.[10]

Some educators worry that disclosure of test answers will help so-called "coaching" schools, which specialize in preparing students to take college entrance and other standardized tests. On the other hand, the effectiveness of these schools has been questioned. The College Board and the Educational Testing Service maintain that coaching or "cramming" does little good because the tests measure general aptitude and skills developed over years of learning. However, a study of two coaching schools in the Boston area published last year by the Federal Trade Commission indicated that coaching might help certain underachievers who do well in school but who do not perform well on standardized tests.[11]

Continued Concern Over Drop in Test Scores

SAT scores have been declining for nearly two decades, although the drop has leveled off somewhat in the last few years *(see box, p. 145)*. The average score on the verbal section of the test declined from 478 in 1962-63 to 426 in 1978-79. The average score on the math section dropped from 502 in 1962-63 to 466 in 1978-79. The tests are scored on a scale from 200 to 800. From 1972 to 1979 the proportion of college-bound students scoring in the 600 to 800 range declined to 7 percent from 11 percent on the verbal section and to 15 percent from 17 percent on the math section.

Scores on tests administered by the American College Testing Program also have fallen in recent years. The average composite score of the ACT tests, which are taken by some 900,000 high school students annually in English, math, social studies and natural sciences, declined from 19.9 in 1969-70 to 18.6 in 1978-79. The ACT scale ranges from 1 to 36.

Concerned about the trend, the College Entrance Examination Board set up an advisory panel headed by former Secretary of Labor Willard Wirtz in 1975 to look into the test-score decline. The panel's report, issued in August 1977, found no single force or closely related set of forces responsible for the decline. The panel concluded that there were two stages in the decline — one between 1963 and 1970, and the other after 1970. The first decline was caused by "compositional" changes in the student population taking the tests, the Wirtz panel said. Each year between 1963 and 1970, those taking the tests "included larger

---

[10] Writing in *The New York Times,* Aug. 15, 1979.

[11] "Effects of Coaching on Standardized Examinations," Federal Trade Commission, Bureau of Consumer Protection, March 1979.

National Test Scores

School Year	SAT[1] Score Averages		ACT[2] Score Averages
	Verbal	Mathematical	Composite
1962-63	478	502	NA[3]
1963-64	475	498	NA[3]
1964-65	473	498	19.9
1965-66	471	496	20.0
1966-67	467	495	19.4
1967-68	466	494	19.0
1968-69	462	491	19.4
1969-70	460	488	19.9
1970-71	454	487	19.2
1971-72	450	482	19.1
1972-73	443	481	19.2
1973-74	440	478	18.9
1974-75	437	473	18.6
1975-76	429	470	18.3
1976-77	429	471	18.4
1977-78	429	469	18.5
1978-79	426	466	18.6

[1] Scholastic Aptitude Test. Scale ranges from 200 to 800.
[2] American College Testing Program. Scale ranges from 1 to 36.
[3] Not Available.

Source: College Entrance Examination Board and the American College Testing Program.

proportions of characteristically lower-scoring groups of students" — who were identified mainly as children of poor or black families and girls, who average lower scores on the math section. "This pulled the overall average down."[12]

The post-1970 decline, the panel reported, probably was caused by many factors, including: (1) the movement away from basics and to elective courses, especially in English, (2) "clearly observable evidence of diminished seriousness of purpose and attention to mastery of skills and knowledge in the learning process as it proceeds in the schools, the home, and the society generally," (3) higher divorce rates, (4) the prevalence of television watching and (5) an "apparent diminution in young people's learning motivation."

U.S. colleges have adjusted to the declining test scores by lowering their own admissions requirements. Approximately 43 percent of the schools responding to the College Board-AACRAO survey said that they expected higher admissions test scores from applicants in 1970 than they did in 1978. Declining scores on college entrance examinations have been interpreted

---

[12] College Entrance Examination Board, "On Further Examination: Report of the Advisory Panel on the Scholastic Aptitude Test Score Decline," 1977, p. 13.

by many to mean that the quality of American education is slipping. A study conducted by the National Association of Secondary School Principals found that students scored considerably higher SAT scores at schools that stressed academic courses such as mathematics, foreign languages, English and physical science than students at schools that experimented with new approaches in curriculum content. The schools across the country where SAT scores rose, the study found, "took certain initiatives or else maintained some specific 'standards' that they considered important to the success of their college-bound students."[13]

Changing Admissions Criteria

UNTIL the late 19th century, most American colleges maintained their own special entrance requirements and prescribed their own courses of study for prospective students. Many established preparatory academies to help youngsters get ready for college studies. If the college did not have its own academy, college-bound students enrolled in another academy or worked with a private tutor who "fitted" them for the college's requirements. Entrance examinations consisted of the college president and several faculty members questioning the candidate on his studies in Latin, Greek and mathematics — the essential ingredients of a classical education. The examinations often went from dawn to dusk, with only a short break for lunch. According to education historian Harold S. Wechsler, "the decision to admit a student . . . was determined by the quality of his answers, the college's financial picture, and not infrequently on the kindliness of a faculty member."[14] As subjects such as geography, English grammar, algebra and history were added to the entrance requirements, many colleges replaced the oral examinations with a battery of written tests.

Colleges sought to strengthen their position in American society by portraying themselves as "capstones" of a system "from which the next generation of American leaders would emerge." To succeed, they needed cooperation from the private academies and later the public high schools in tailoring secondary school curriculum to fit college requirements. But the diversity of college entrance requirements made the task difficult. Wilson Farrand, headmaster of Newark Academy, explained the problem in a speech he gave in 1895: "Princeton and Columbia call

---

[13] National Association of Secondary School Principals, "Guidelines for Improving SAT Scores," 1978, p. 4.

[14] Harold S. Wechsler, *The Qualified Student* (1977), p. 7.

for six books of the *Aeneid;* Yale requires, in addition, the *Ecologues.* These do not count for maximum standing at Princeton unless combined with the *Georgics* . . . Princeton requires Latin of candidates for one course, but not for the others. Yale demands it of all, Columbia of none."[15]

While colleges and high schools in the East continued to bicker over entrance requirements, the University of Michigan pioneered a new system of accepting all graduates of high schools that had been accredited by a team of faculty inspectors. The plan was championed by Harry S. Frieze, a professor who served as acting president of the university in 1870-71. Frieze modeled the Michigan plan on the German gymnasia, secondary schools which prepared students for the university. Many of those who supported admission by certificate, Wechsler wrote, saw it as a "potential solution for solving a basic problem faced by most American colleges in the 19th century — the need to maintain and if possible to increase enrollments."[16] Only 5 percent of American 17-year-olds graduated from high school in 1890, and only a fraction of this group went on to college. Many colleges adopted the certificate system with the expectation that more students would seek admission once demanding entrance examinations were dropped. As more institutions joined the movement, regional associations were established to assume responsibility for inspecting and accrediting secondary schools.

By the turn of the century, the certificate system had become the most popular method of regulating college admissions. It gained strongest acceptance in the Midwest, where the movement began. Resistance was strongest in the older, elite colleges of New England and the Middle Atlantic States. "Such institutions," Wechsler wrote, "opposed certification because it was new and they revered traditions; because it threatened their domination of the high schools. . . ; and because it implied that they were in competition for students, something their high enrollments did not support in fact and their high self-estimate did not allow in principle."[17] In time, however, all of the Ivy League schools except Harvard, Princeton and Yale joined the system.

Estabishment of the College Board in 1900

The elite colleges were never comfortable with the certificate system, but neither were they satisfied with widely divergent

---

[15] From Farrand's inaugural address as president of the Schoolmaster's Association of New York and vicinity, Oct. 12, 1895. His topic was "The Reform of College Entrance Requirements."

[16] Wechsler, *op. cit.,* p. 20.

[17] *Ibid.,* p. 57.

standards for college entrance. Presidents Nicholas Murray But-
ler of Columbia and Charles W. Eliot of Harvard led the campaign to bring about closer cooperation between institutions of
higher learning and secondary schools, while keeping the final
decision on admissions with the colleges. Their efforts cul-
minated in the creation of the College Entrance Examination
Board in 1900.[18]

The College Board, as it came to be known, supplied standardized entrance examinations to its members. Only 12 schools
were members at the beginning: Barnard, Bryn Mawr, Columbia, Cornell, Johns Hopkins, New York University, University of
Pennsylvania, Rutgers, Swarthmore, Union, Vassar and Wom-
en's College of Baltimore. Gradually the board attracted more
members, who saw in it the chance to reach a larger and more
varied group of students. Examinations soon were available to
students throughout the nation. By 1910, even "The Big Three"
— Harvard, Yale and Princeton — had joined the fold.

The original College Board tests were essay examinations that
measured a student's retention of specific facts. But educators
soon began to question whether such tests identified candidates
who would succeed in college. Following World War I, the College Board became interested in testing programs developed by
the government to measure soldiers' aptitude for various assign-
ments. In 1926 the board administered its first aptitude test, the
SAT, a multiple choice exam covering a wide variety of topics.
The goal of the aptitude test was to measure "future ability"
rather than "past mastery." The tests were supposed to "reveal
the broad expanse of a student's knowledge, not the minute details of his preparation."[19] The board continued to offer the
older essay examinations, but most colleges preferred the new
SAT. Most of the older exams were dropped during World War
II and never resumed.

By 1946, the College Board had expanded its testing program
far beyond college entrance examinations. Among its clients
were the U.S. Department of State, the Bureau of Naval Personnel, the U.S. Naval Academy, the Coast Guard Academy and
the National Administrative Board for the Pepsi-Cola Scholar-
ships. Many members felt the board had strayed too far from its
original mandate to provide college entrance examinations. On
Dec. 19, 1947, the board, in cooperation with the Carnegie
Foundation for the Advancement of Teaching and the American
Council on Education, established the Educational Testing Service (ETS). The new organization was to assume responsibility

---

[18] See Claude M. Fuess, *The College Board, Its First Fifty Years* (1967).

[19] Wechsler, *op. cit.*, pp. 247-248.

An Insider's View of College Admissions

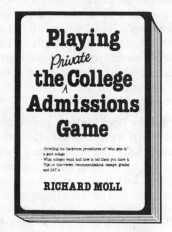

Playing *Private* **the College Admissions Game**

Unveiling the backroom procedures of "who gets in" a good college
What colleges want and how to tell them you have it.
Tips on interviews, recommendations, essays, grades and SAT's

RICHARD MOLL

"A college simply can't apply a uniform standard of 'academic excellence' and end up accidently with an adequate showing of legacy students [children of alumni] and minorities, with a basketball team, and with geographic distribution," writes Richard Moll, director of admissions at Vassar College, in his book, *Playing the Private College Admissions Game* (1979).

Moll said that most admissions offices divide candidates into five or more categories with separate standards for each group. "The Merit Scholar, the extraordinarily talented violinist, the . . . alumnus' son, the nifty all-round kid, and the black are not going to nudge one another out of the running: They're competing against others of like interest and talent for that particular group's fair share of the class."

Moll said class rank and the degree of difficulty of high school courses are the prime factors in evaluating a student's academic potential. But entrance examinations are important too. "The problem is that no other single means of appraisal is so uniform — high school grade patterns differ from school to school. . . . So, by default, College Board (or ACT) scores become a universal language for defining the quality of a candidate or a class."

for developing all the tests formerly handled by the board itself. The board would focus its attention entirely on the tests used by high schools and colleges. It would have broad policy authority over the content of the exams and also handle such matters as the location and frequency of various tests.

Efforts to Expand U.S. College Population

A report published by the President's Commission on Higher Education in 1946 noted that only a fraction of those who could benefit from higher education actually were enrolled in colleges. "American colleges must envision a much larger role for higher education in the national life," the commission stated. "They can no longer consider themselves merely the instrument for producing an intellectual elite; they must become the means by which every citizen, youth and adult, is enabled and encouraged to carry his education, formal and informal, as far as his native capacities permit."

For 20 years following the end of World War II American colleges and universities experienced unparalleled growth and expansion. The beginning of this new era in higher education came with the passage of the Servicemen's Readjustment Act of 1944 — the G.I. Bill — "the largest scholarship program in the nation's history." The federal government provided veterans who were enrolled as full-time students with living allowances and made direct payments to the institution for tuition, fees, and laboratory, library and other normal school costs.

The coming of age of the "baby boom" generation born after World War II shot college enrollment up in the 1960s. Between 1959-60 and 1969-70 enrollment more than doubled, rising from 3,471,000 to some 7,978,000. Not only was there a large increase in the number of persons of college age, but the proportion going to college also rose. By 1970, 34 percent of the 18-21 age group were enrolled in degree-credit programs in higher education, compared with 23 percent in 1960, 15 percent in 1950 and 11 percent in 1940.

The social pressures to go to college increased enormously during the 1960s. Higher education not only was seen as the most likely path to economic success and individual fulfillment, but a steady rise in per capita income throughout the decade meant that more parents could afford to send their children to college than ever before. And as more and more persons obtained degrees, employers began recruiting college graduates for jobs that had formerly gone to persons with a high school education.

At the same time that a college degree became an essential component of the American Dream, it became more difficult to obtain. As enrollments soared in the late 1950s and the 1960s, many private institutions, and some public ones, began to limit enrollment and raise admission standards. Increased emphasis was placed on a student's performance on national college aptitude tests, including the Scholastic Aptitude Test (SAT) administered by the College Board. So great was the demand for student ability screening that another national testing service, the American College Testing Program (ACT), was founded in 1959 in Iowa City, Iowa.

One of the most dynamic developments in higher education during this period was the growth of two-year community colleges. Vocationally oriented junior colleges had been around since the mid-19th century, but they remained a minor facet of American education until the late 1950s. By the mid-1960s these colleges, by now being called community colleges, were opening at a rate of about one a week. In the 1959-60 school year, some 640,500 students were enrolled in two-year colleges. A decade later, the number had grown to almost two million full- and part-time students, nearly 30 percent of all undergraduates in the nation. The rapid advance of community colleges was attributed to their open-admissions policies, their geographic distribution across the country, and their usually low tuition fees.

Future Enrollment Patterns

FOR MUCH of its history, the story of American higher education was one of growth and expansion. But times have changed. After more than a quarter-century of uninterrupted growth, college enrollments started levelling off in the mid-1970s. The number of people enrolled in the nation's colleges and universities is expected to decline in the 1980s *(see graph, p. 153).* This view is supported by Census Bureau projections that the country's college-age population will shrink 18 percent between 1980 and 1990, with most of the drop — 11 percent — occurring during the first half of the decade. By 1985, there will be 1.7 million fewer 18-to-21-year olds than in 1980.

The projected enrollment drop threatens many institutions with both financial and educational problems. From an economic standpoint, colleges may be faced with declining tuition payments at a time of steadily increasing costs. Many small private colleges could go out of business.[20] Public colleges and universities probably will face the loss of some programs as a result of federal and state budget cuts. Even the most financially stable institutions may have to reduce their programs and faculties if the number of students declines significantly.

Faced with the prospects of waning enrollment for the remainder of the decade, colleges and universities have begun to broaden their recruiting efforts. Many are aiming their pitch at adults. Students 25 and older numbered 1.7 million and accounted for 22 percent of the campus population in 1970. By 1975 these figures had jumped to 34 percent and 3.7 million and, according to a Census Bureau estimate, four of every 10 collegians may be above 25 by 1985 if current enrollment rates by age continue at the prevailing pace.

A report published recently by the Carnegie Council on Policy Studies in Higher Education said that projected increases in the number of older students during the next two decades will offset about 9 percent of the projected drop in the number of students aged 18-25. "Participation rates for adults with prior college attendance may rise to even higher levels than past practice might indicate . . . ," the report concluded, "because of the great

---

[20] See "Future of Private Colleges," *E.R.R.,* 1976 Vol. I, pp. 305-322.

competition of many to get ahead within the bulge of young adults, because of the desire of some to change jobs in the face of this competition, and because of the impulse of a few to escape the competition by attention to non-vocational interests."[21]

Robert Hawkes Jr., dean of the division of continuing education at George Mason University in Fairfax City, Va., calls the burgeoning of adult education "the quiet revolution," as opposed to the "turbulent" era of college demonstrations in the 1960s. He believes the latest revolution "will have an even larger impact" than the earlier one. "For the most part," he said recently, adults "are incredibly good students," something U.S. educators first learned when veterans began enrolling in colleges after World War II with the aid of the G.I. Bill.[22]

The Wall Street Journal recently reported that 500,000 executives take advanced management courses every year, ranging from weekend seminars to degree-granting programs lasting a year or more. Many colleges send their professors off campus to teach executives on their home ground. Some educators have strong reservations about the off-campus programs, however. Often they provide "little more than poor quality education delivered anywhere to any student for monetary gain," said Kay Anderson, director of an accrediting agency for schools in California and Hawaii.[23]

Increase in Foreign Student Enrollments

The crisis in Iran and President Carter's subsequent order to deport some Iranian students has heightened the nation's awareness of foreign students in American universities. Their numbers have increased fivefold over the last two decades, from 50,000 in 1960 to more than 260,000 today. In the past, colleges admitted foreign students primarily to add to the diversity of campus life. Today the motive often is money. Richard Farmer, chairman of the department of international business at Indiana University in Bloomington, has calculated that the average foreign student spends $10,000 a year for tuition, fees, books, travel and other costs.[24]

Students from oil exporting countries have come to the United States in increasing numbers in recent years. Those from nations in the Organization of Petroleum Exporting Countries

---

[21] "Three Thousand Futures: The Next 20 Years for Higher Education," Final Report of the Carnegie Council on Policy Studies in Higher Education, 1980, p. 37.

[22] Quoted by James T. Yenckel in *The Washington Post*, March 17, 1980.

[23] Quoted by Andy Pasztor and Rich Jaroslovsky in *The Wall Street Journal*, May 21, 1979.

[24] Quoted by Edward B. Fiske in a series of stories on recruitment of foreign students appearing in *The New York Times*, Feb. 24-25, 1980.

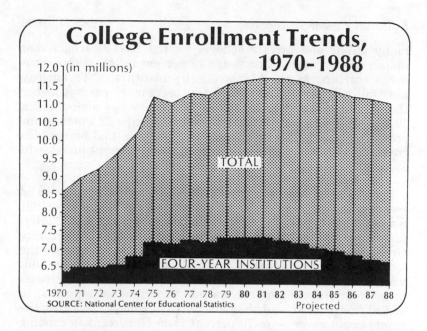

College Enrollment Trends, 1970-1988

12.0 (in millions)
11.5
11.0
10.5
10.0
9.5
9.0
8.5
8.0
7.5
7.0
6.5

TOTAL

FOUR-YEAR INSTITUTIONS

1970 71 72 73 74 75 76 77 78 79 80 81 82 83 84 85 86 87 88

SOURCE: National Center for Educational Statistics   Projected

(OPEC) make up about a third of all foreign students compared to only 12 percent in 1971-72. Iran leads the list of foreign nations sending students to the United States, with at least 45,000 studying in this country. Nigeria is second with 16,200. Saudi Arabia, Venezuela and Mexico each send more than 5,000. Many foreign students in the United States come from South and East Asia. Taiwan now has about 15,400 students here, Hong Kong and Japan more than 10,000, and Thailand more than 5,000. China, which is just beginning to sample the U.S. college market, has sent about 1,000 students so far, including the son of Deng Xiaoping, the senior Deputy Prime Minister.

Graduate students make up about 44 percent of the foreign college students. The National Academy of Science reported in 1977 that foreign students received 42 percent of the doctoral degrees awarded by American institutions in engineering and 25 percent of those in physics and mathematics. There is some concern that foreign students are taking college seats away from Americans; but it is pointed out that there is a shortage of U.S. applicants for many graduate programs which attract foreign students such as civil engineering. In the elite schools, entrance requirements usually are much stricter for foreigners than for U.S. students.

Problems Created by Rising Tuition Costs

Getting into college may be easier in the 1980s, but paying for it is likely to become more difficult. College costs rose nearly 70 percent in the last decade, and inflation is expected to push them higher in the years ahead. Tuition increases announced at many public and private colleges for the 1980-81 school year match or even exceed last year's 13 percent inflation rate. Students enrolling at the Massachusetts Institute of Technology next fall will pay $6,200 tuition for the year, 17 percent higher than the previous year. Stanford University has announced a 12.3 percent increase to $6,285 a year, Harvard a 13.2 percent increase to $6,000, the University of Chicago a 13.3 percent increase to $5,100 and Clark University a 16.1 percent increase to $5,400.[25]

Proposals to increase federal aid to college students are in jeopardy as the president and Congress seek to balance the 1981 federal budget. Administration officials have branded as "inflationary" a bill that would raise Basic Educational Opportunity Grants (BEOGs) by $2.1 billion in fiscal 1981 and increase the total cost of federal student aid to $11 billion by 1985. The bill, which was approved by the House in 1979, would allow increases in both the maximum cash awards to individual students, to $2,520 from $1,800, and the percentage of college costs that the grants could cover — to 70 percent from 50 percent in existing law. A similar bill now is before the Senate Labor and Human Resources Education Subcommittee.[26]

Congress has been debating new approaches to federal student aid. Legislation to provide federal tuition tax credits to parents gathered broad support in both houses of Congress in 1978, but the measure died after President Carter said he would veto it. The administration opposed the measure on the ground that it would benefit all families regardless of economic need rather than concentrating resources on low-income families.[27]

Some educators believe the primary burden of paying for a college education should fall on the student, not his or her family. John Silber, president of Boston University, has proposed a plan to provide tuition advances of up to $5,000 a year, up to a total of $15,000, for students who successfully complete their freshman year of college. After graduation the student would begin paying back the tuition advance at the rate of 2 percent of his gross annual income. There would be no interest, per se, but the student would owe a 50 percent surcharge which would go into an endowment fund to support the program. A person who borrowed the maximum amount of $15,000 would have to pay an additional $7,500. Silber justified the extra fee by pointing to Census Bureau figures which show that the average male college

[25] Reported by Jack Magarrell in "Many Colleges Plan 2-Digit Increases in Tuition to Keep Up With Inflation," *The Chronicle of Higher Education,* March 3, 1980.

[26] See Congressional Quarterly *Weekly Report,* March 1, 1980, p. 630.

[27] See "College Tuition Costs," *E.R.R.,* 1978 Vol. I, pp. 141-160 and *1978 CQ Almanac,* p. 248.

graduate earns about $232,000 more during a lifetime than a male high school graduate. Critics of the proposal contend that such a large debt — $22,500 to cover the maximum advance and surcharge — is too great a burden for most graduates to carry.

Opportunities in New Admissions Climate

The coming decade may fulfill the mandate of the 1946 President's Commission on Higher Education which envisioned a system of higher education in which every citizen could participate. Demographic trends may do more for the cause of universal college education than the best laid plans of educators or government officials. The Carnegie Council predicts that during the next 20 years students "will be recruited more actively, admitted more readily, retained more assiduously, counseled more attentively, graded more considerately, financed more adequately, taught more conscientiously, placed in jobs more insistently, and the curriculum will be more tailored to their tastes."[28]

Some educators wonder what the trend toward mass college education will mean for academic standards. There already are complaints that today's students are unprepared for college-level studies and that many lack even basic skills in English and mathematics. Theodore L. Gross, former dean of humanities at the City College of New York during that institution's experiment with "open admissions" and now provost of the Capital Campus of Pennsylvania State University, has called for a National Center for Literacy which would explore ways to ensure that high school students are well grounded in English and writing skills before they reach college.[29]

Many educators feel that the challenge of mass higher education can become an opportunity for colleges and other institutions of higher learning to expand their own horizons, a chance to rethink the American educational system. Colleges have adapted to the needs of new groups of students in the past, and they can do so again, it is argued. As the competition for college entrance subsides, admissions officers and professors may be able to spend more time and effort on developing programs to meet the diverse needs of the student population. Admissions tests might be used to learn more about applicants rather than as a tool to select or reject them. The 1980s, it seems, is a crossroad for higher education. The choices that are made will determine the fate of a generation of students and of the colleges themselves.

---

[28] "Three Thousand Futures," *op. cit.*, p. 54.

[29] Theodore L. Gross, *Academic Turmoil* (1980), pp. 166-221.

Selected Bibliography

Books

Barton, David W. Jr., Ed., *Marketing of Higher Education,* Jossey-Bass Inc., 1978.

Fuess, Claude M., *The College Board: The First Fifty Years,* College Entrance Examination Board, 1967.

Gross, Theodore L., *Academic Turmoil,* Anchor Press-Doubleday, 1980.

Marland, Sidney P. Jr., *The College Board and the Twentieth Century,* College Entrance Examination Board, 1975.

Moll, Richard, *Playing the Private College Admissions Game,* Times Books, 1979.

Sacks, Herbert S., et. al., *Hurdles: The Admissions Dilemma in American Higher Education,* Atheneum, 1978.

Wechsler, Harold S., *The Qualified Student,* John Wiley & Sons, Inc., 1977.

Articles

Chase, Alston, "Financing A College Education," *Atlantic,* April 1980.

"Controversy In Congress Over Federal Student-Aid Policy," *Congressional Digest,* January 1979.

Fallows, James, "The Tests and the 'Brightest': How Fair Are The College Boards?" *Atlantic,* February 1980.

Farnsworth, Kent A., "Selling the Student Consumer," *Change,* November-December 1979.

Fiske, Edward B., "The Marketing of the Colleges," *Atlantic,* October 1979.

Jencks, Christopher, "Why Students Aren't Learning," *The Center Magazine,* July-August 1979.

Nader, Ralph, "Student Power 101," *Change,* November-December 1979.

Sewall, Gil, et. al., "Tests: How Good? How Fair?," *Time,* Feb. 18, 1980.

Smith, R. Jeffrey, " 'Truth-in-Testing' Attracts Diverse Support," *Science,* September 1979.

Reports and Studies

Carnegie Council on Policy Studies in Higher Education:"Opportunity For Women in Higher Education," 1973; "Selective Admissions in Higher Education," 1977; "Three Thousand Futures: The Next 20 Years For Higher Education," Final Report, 1980.

College Board-American Association of College Registrars and Admissions Officers, "Survey of Admissions Policies, Practices and Procedures," Sept. 20, 1979.

College Board, "On Further Examination: Report of the Advisory Panel on the Scholastic Aptitude Test Score Decline," 1977.

Editorial Research Reports: "College Recruiting," 1974 Vol. II, p. 61; "Future of Private Colleges," 1976 Vol. I, p. 305; "College Tuition Costs," 1978 Vol I, p. 141; "Competency Tests," 1978 Vol. II, p. 601.

Federal Trade Commission, Bureau of Consumer Protection, "Effects of Coaching on Standardized Admission Examinations," Revised Statistical Analysis, March 1979.

Nairn, Allan and Associates, "The Reign of ETS-The Ralph Nader Report on the Educational Testing Service," January 1980.

156

Violence in the Family

by

Sandra Stencel

Apr. 27
1 9 7 9

Editor's Note: There were 788,844 official reports of child maltreatment (involving a total of 1.2 million children) in the United States in 1980, according to the American Humane Association in Denver, Colo. This represented a 91 percent increase from 1976. The U.S. Supreme Court ruled March 24, 1982, that states had to have clear and convincing proof of child abuse or neglect before removing children from the custody of their natural parents.

VIOLENCE IN THE FAMILY

THE IMAGE of the family as a refuge from the strains and stresses of the outside world is one most Americans hold dear. Our unwillingness to abandon this idealized picture of family life, despite rising divorce rates and other signs of family discord,[1] is perhaps an indication that the American family is here to stay. This optimistic assessment of the future of the family draws general agreement. But there also seems to be a growing recognition that this idyllic concept of family life has contributed to the conspiracy of silence that, until very recently, surrounded the problem of violence in the family.

Evidence of violent confrontations among family members, especially extreme cases of child abuse and neglect, were never completely ignored by law enforcement personnel, social workers, psychologists or the news media. But the tendency was to view these cases as abnormalities, as exceptions to the usual state of affairs. Family violence also was seen as primarily a working-class phenomenon. In recent years, however, it has become increasingly apparent that violence in the family is a much more serious problem than many realized — or were willing to admit. Consider these statistics:

> In 1977, according to the FBI Uniform Crime Reports, nearly 20 percent of all murder victims in the United States were related to the assailants. About half of these intra-family murders were husband-wife killings.[2]

> In any one year, according to one study,[3] approximately 1.8 million wives are beaten by their husbands. Over one-fourth of all American couples engage in at least one violent episode during their relationship.

> Over one million children are abused each year, physically, sexually or through neglect, the Department of Health, Education and Welfare (HEW) reports. About 240,000 children are victims of physical abuse and at least 2,000 of them die of their injuries.[4]

---

[1] See "The Changing American Family," *E.R.R.*, 1977 Vol. I, pp. 413-432.
[2] U.S. Department of Justice, "FBI Uniform Crime Reports: Crime in the United States, 1977," Oct. 18, 1978, p. 9.
[3] See Murray A. Straus, "Wife Beating: How Common and Why?" *Victimology: An International Journal*, November 1977, p. 445.
[4] U.S. Department of Health, Education and Welfare, "New Light on an Old Problem: 9 Questions and Answers on Child Abuse and Neglect," 1978, p. 5.

"The family is both the most loving and supportive of human groups and also by far the most physically violent group or institution except for the police or the military during a war," Professor Murray A. Straus of the University of New Hampshire said at a meeting of the American Psychological Association in Toronto, Aug. 29, 1978. "Violence in the home is a far more serious problem than violence in the streets, in the classrooms, or anywhere else."

Violence within the family does not necessarily have to involve physical abuse. While Professor Straus notes that "the most common of all forms of intra-family violence" is the physical punishment of children *(see p. 169)*, psychologists and sociologists also are beginning to recognize the toll so-called "emotional violence" takes on family members. The most common tactics in emotional warfare are the withholding of sex, love or money. An increasingly popular strategy is the "honesty or openness maneuver, where being brutally frank is often times an excuse for being brutal."[5]

Increased Attention From the Government

In recent years the problem of domestic violence has been receiving more attention. Child abuse and wife battering have been the subject of numerous newspaper and magazine articles, radio and television talk shows and even a few made-for-television movies. Social service agencies, church groups, schools, colleges and other organizations are offering courses, seminars and lectures on various aspects of the problem.

The women's movement has encouraged battered women to speak more openly about their predicament and to demand protection from the police and the courts. Some police departments are beginning to train officers in family crisis intervention. Social workers are being trained better to detect domestic violence when rendering other services. And prosecutors show a new willingness to bring domestic violence cases to trial.

Hearings have been held at the state and local level to measure the prevalence of domestic violence and to consider such remedies as legislation and coordination of social services. In the past decade most states have strengthened their laws to encourage prompt reporting of suspected cases of child battering. In many states, telephone "hot lines" have been set up to assist the public in reporting suspected cases of child abuse and to offer advice to victims of domestic violence *(see p. 173)*. Emergency shelters for battered wives and their dependents are being opened in a growing number of communities.

---

[5] Remarks of Barbara O'Connor, a New York social worker, at a seminar on emotional violence within the family held Nov. 18, 1978, at the New School for Social Research in New York.

Murders in the Family

Year	All reported murders	Spouse killing spouse	Parent killing child	Other relative killings
		(in percentages)		
1969	14,680	13.1	3.7	8.4
1970	15,910	12.1	3.1	8.1
1971	17,680	12.8	3.5	8.4
1972	18,570	12.5	2.9	8.9
1973	19,530	12.3	3.2	7.7
1974	20,600	12.1	2.7	8.0
1975	20,510	11.5	3.0	7.9
1976	18,780	*	*	*
1977	19,120	10.6	3.1	5.3

*In 1976 available figures show that a total of 27.2 percent of all reported murders were by relatives.

Source: FBI Uniform Crime Reports

Growing awareness of the problem also prompted action at the federal level. The Child Abuse Prevention and Treatment Act, passed by Congress on Jan. 31, 1974, authorized $85 million over a three-year period for federal aid to programs for the prevention, identification and treatment of child abuse. At least half of the funds were assigned to demonstration programs and to training programs for professionals involved in child abuse work. The National Center on Child Abuse and Neglect was created by the Child Abuse Prevention and Treatment Act to administer these funds. The National Center, within HEW, also is responsible for studying the incidence of child abuse nationwide and for maintaining a central clearinghouse of information on child abuse and neglect.

In 1977 Congress extended the Child Abuse Prevention and Treatment Act for two years, through fiscal 1979. The reauthorization bill broadened the definition of child abuse under the bill to include "sexual abuse and exploitation." Some $2 million was authorized in fiscal 1978 and again in 1979 for programs and projects designed to prevent, identify and treat sexual abuse of children. In a report issued in August 1978, the National Center on Child Abuse and Neglect estimated that the current annual incidence of sexual abuse of children is between 60,000 and 100,000 cases a year.[6]

Last year the Senate passed but the House voted down separate bills to establish a new federal program for financing spouse-abuse shelters and other community activities intended to prevent family violence and treat its victims. The bills pro-

[6] National Center on Child Abuse and Neglect, "Child Sexual Abuse: Incest, Assault, and Sexual Exploitation," August 1978, p. 3.

posed to establish a National Center on Domestic Violence within HEW.[7] Women's groups, pushing for reintroduction of the bills this year, cite the continuing need for additional federal funding for spouse abuse shelters.[8] As late as 1976, only 30 such houses were known to exist. By 1978, over 170 shelters were operating in the United States, according to a survey conducted by the Center for Women Policy Studies in Washington, D.C.[9]

Police Response to Wife-Battering Cases

It is generally agreed that available statistics greatly underestimate the extent of violence within the family. Many cases of child abuse and spouse battering still go unreported, even though every state now requires physicians to report suspected cases of child abuse. In most states the reporting requirements also apply to other medical personnel, including nurses, dentists, interns, coroners and medical examiners. Since 1973, according to the National Center on Child Abuse and Neglect, many states have broadened their reporting requirements to cover non-medical professionals, including teachers and law-enforcement and child-care personnel.[10]

States and localities have been slower to respond to the problem of spouse abuse. Police authorities often are reluctant to get involved in such cases since wife beating traditionally has been thought of not as a crime, but as a private marital squabble. Police indifference is thought to have contributed to the reluctance of many battered wives to even call the police. The FBI has said that wife battering may be the most underreported crime in the nation.

Police intervention in domestic violence can be dangerous. About 20 percent of the deaths and 40 percent of injuries suffered by the police occur when officers seek to intervene in such cases. But the primary reason police are reluctant to get involved in domestic fights, according to James Bannon, executive deputy chief of the Detroit Police Department, "is because we

[7] The Senate bill was introduced by Alan Cranston, D-Calif.; the House version was sponsored by Reps. George Miller, D-Calif., Lindy Boggs, D-La., Newton Steers, R-Md., and Barbara Mikulski, D-Md. See *CQ Weekly Report* of May 27, 1978, p. 1335, and Sept. 16, 1978, p. 2485.

[8] Some federal funding for shelters is provided under Title XX of the Social Security Act. Title XX, which took effect Oct. 1, 1975, authorized federal payments to the states for provision of social services directed at the goals of (1) economic self-support, (2) personal self-sufficiency, (3) prevention or correction of neglect of children or adults and preservation of families, (4) prevention of inappropriate institutional care through community-based care programs and (5) provision of institutional care where appropriate.

[9] Center for Women Policy Studies, "Programs Providing Services to Battered Women," April 1978. The Center for Women Policy Studies received two grants from the Law Enforcement Assistance Administration (LEAA) to develop a clearinghouse and a newsletter to gather and share information on domestic violence, child sexual abuse and rape. The center recently received another LEAA grant to provide assistance to LEAA-funded Family Violence Programs in 17 communities across the nation.

[10] National Center on Child Abuse and Neglect, "Child Abuse and Neglect: State Reporting Laws," May 1978, pp. 7-8. See also "Child Abuse," *E.R.R.*, 1976 Vol. I, pp. 65-84.

Battered Husbands

"The most unreported crime is not wife beating — it's husband beating," according to University of Delaware sociologist Suzanne Steinmetz. "Unless a man is battered to the degree where he requires medical attention, he is not going to report it." Extrapolating from her studies of domestic quarreling in New Castle County, Del., Steinmetz has estimated that each year at least 250,000 American husbands are severely thrashed by their wives.

"Most battered men are too ashamed to admit they've been beaten by their wives," Roger Langley and Richard C. Levy noted in their book *Wife Beating: The Silent Crisis* (1977). "The humiliation a battered woman suffers is multiplied enormously for a man who must stand before a police sergeant and file a complaint. Not many men have the courage to face the snickers, innuendos, and open sarcasm inherent in this situation."

Langley and Levy also observed that there are few places a battered man can go for help. "When he does reach out," they wrote, "or if circumstances propel the family problem into the public arena, a man can find his life bewildering and frustrating. He can conclude as easily as does the battered wife that the police, the courts, the clergy, and the social-service agencies are all stacked against him."

do not know how to cope with them."[11] To overcome this problem, a growing number of police departments are forming specially trained units. In Atlanta, for example, police are taught through role-playing to defuse family fights by projecting a calm, mediating manner rather than the aggressive posture of an arresting officer.

A training guide on wife beating published by the International Association of Chiefs of Police in 1976 reflected changing police attitudes toward domestic violence. It urged police to distinguish between situations where there is a threat of violence, and where mediation might be effective, and situations where violence already has occurred. "Where an attack has already taken place," it stated, "the police officer must be prepared to conduct an assault investigation. . . . 'Family disturbances' and 'wife beatings' should not be viewed synonymously; nor should wife abuse be considered a victimless crime or solely a manifestation of a poor marraige. A wife beating is foremost an assault — a crime that must be investigated."

Several states have modified their laws to make it easier to arrest wife batterers. An Oregon law that took effect in October 1977 states that a police officer called to a domestic disturbance must take the assailant into custody when the officer has reasonable cause to believe an assault has occurred or a person

---

[11] Quoted by Joan Potter in "Police and the Battered Wife: The Search for Understanding," *Police Magazine,* September 1978, p. 41.

has been placed in fear of injury. A similar law went into effect in Minnesota in April 1978. Until that time Minnesota police could make an arrest for a misdemeanor assault only if the assault was committed in their presence. Under the new law an officer can make an arrest for a domestic assault he did not witness if he has probable cause to believe it happened within the preceding four hours or if there is visible injury to the victim.

Many changes in police attitudes and in domestic violence laws are attributed to a class-action suit filed in December 1976 against the New York City Police Department. The suit was filed on behalf of 71 wives who accused the police of denying them assistance after they reported being assaulted by their husbands. In June 1978 the police department agreed in an out-of-court settlement to arrest wife beaters when there was reasonable cause to believe the men had committed the crime. New York City Counsel Allan G. Schwartz said the new stipulation did not change existing law but "recognizes that, in practice in the past, married women in assault cases have been treated differently from unmarried women."[12]

The out-of-court settlement stipulated that the police department would send one or more officers in response to every call from a woman who said that her husband had assaulted her or was threatening her with assault. The police also agreed to inform a battered wife of her rights; to protect the wife or aid her in getting medical help if she needs it; and to try to locate the assailant if he had left the scene.

One reason police have been reluctant to respond to wife battering cases is that many women are reluctant to prosecute their husbands. Only about 2 percent of the accused males are ever prosecuted. Many feminists argue that this is because prosecutors make it very difficult to press charges. "Prosecutors impose extraordinary conditions on a woman complaining of assaults or harassment by her husband or former husband," wrote Marjory D. Fields, a lawyer with the Brooklyn Legal Services Corporation. "After she passes these tests of her intent to prosecute, pleas to minor infractions are accepted and suspended sentences . . . recommended to the court. Judges impose light or suspended sentences even without the prosecutor's suggestion. Thus, the injured wife who persists does not receive the protection of having her assaultive husband jailed."[13]

According to Fields, "prompt and certain punishment" is the only answer to wife abuse. Others believe that traditional prosecution is not always appropriate. Charles Benjamin Schudson, an assistant district attorney in Milwaukee, Wis., said: "Crimi-

---

[12] Quoted in *The New York Times*, June 27, 1978.

[13] Marjory D. Fields, "Representing Battered Wives, or What To Do Until the Police Arrive," *The Family Law Reporter*, April 5, 1977.

nal prosecution is an act of desperation. It's something done when all else has failed. Sometimes it is necessary, sometimes it must be done. But what I'm saying is that . . . criminal prosecution does not solve the problem."[14]

Self-Defense Pleas in Wife-Husband Killings

Frustrated by the criminal justice system, some battered wives have taken the law into their own hands — and many of them have gotten away with it, as a number of press reports indicate:

> Marlene Roan Eagle, a pregnant American Indian in South Dakota, stabbed her husband through the heart after he came at her with a broken broomstick. It was established that he had beaten her on several occasions and, in July 1977, she was acquitted of murder on the ground that she acted in self-defense.
>
> Sharon McNearney was found innocent of murdering her husband in November 1977. The Marquette, Mich., housewife fired a shotgun at him as he walked through the front door. Police described her as a battered wife who had long been abused. Marquette County Circuit Court Judge John E. McDonald said the prosecution failed to prove she had not acted in self-defense.
>
> The same month Evelyn Ware was found not guilty of murdering her husband after pleading self-defense in Superior Court in Orange County, Calif. She shot her husband five times. Evidence of past beatings was used as part of her defense.
>
> In the spring of 1977 a jury in Bellingham, Wash., acquitted Janice Hornbuckle of first-degree murder. One night, after her husband beat her and threatened her at knife-point, she grabbed a shotgun from her teenage son and shot her husband. She had sought police protection on several occasions.
>
> In Chicago, Juan Malonado was shot and killed by his wife, Gloria, after he beat his eight-year-old son with a shoe. The State's Attorney's office ruled there was "insufficient evidence" to warrant her prosecution.
>
> In a well-publicized case in Lansing, Mich., Francine Hughes claimed that years of physical abuse drove her to pour gasoline around her sleeping husband and light it. A jury acquitted her of murder on the ground of temporary insanity.

These and other similar cases have attracted national attention and generated considerable controversy. Indeed, it has been suggested that the acquittals could result in an "open season on men."[15] Despite the controversy, lawyers increasingly are using

---

[14] Interview on "The MacNeil/Lehrer Report," Public Broadcasting System, Oct. 19, 1978.

[15] See "Thirteen Ways to Leave Your Lover," *New Times*, Feb. 6, 1978, p. 6. See also "A Killing Excuse," *Time*, Nov. 28, 1977, p. 108; "The Right to Kill," *Newsweek*, Sept. 1, 1975, p. 69; "Wives Who Batter Back," *Newsweek*, Jan. 30, 1978, p. 54; and "Wives Accused of Slayings Turning to Self-Defense Pleas," *The Washington Post*, Dec. 4, 1977.

Marital Rape

One aspect of spouse abuse that until recently received very little attention is marital rape. That was before the celebrated Rideout case in Oregon. Last October, Greta Rideout, then 23, charged her husband John with rape. Filing such a charge would have been unthinkable and, in fact, impossible until the Oregon legislature changed the state's rape law in 1977 to remove marriage or cohabitation as a defense.

John Rideout was acquitted of the rape charge in January. But that did not end the debate on marital rape. Besides Oregon, at least three other states — New Jersey, Delaware and Iowa — have revised their rape laws to allow women to charge their husbands with sexual assault. Several other states, including California, are considering similar legal changes.

The Rideouts, when last heard from, were granted a divorce after a brief reconciliation.

the self-defense plea in wife-husband murders. Two lawyers associated with the Center for Constitutional Rights in New York last year published a report intended to help attorneys representing women who commit homicide after they or their children have been physically or sexually assaulted.[16] "Ten years ago women didn't talk about being raped," said one of the lawyers, Elizabeth M. Schneider. "Ten years ago women didn't talk about being battered. If they fought back, society and they themselves thought they were wrong to do it; they pleaded guilty and they went to jail. The climate of the times now is that more battered women are ready to say, 'It's either him or me at this moment and I choose me.' You can't really assert self-defense until you feel you have a self to defend; that's what women finally are developing."[17]

In many states, to prove self-defense the defendant has to show a reasonable apprehension of imminent danger of great bodily harm. Lawyers have effectively used evidence of past beatings and threats to show reasonable apprehension, even in cases where the husband's actions at the moment of the killing are inconclusive or negligible. Lawyers also have successfully argued that it is not an unreasonable response for a physically outmatched wife to resort to a lethal weapon such as a gun or a knife if a husband comes at her with his fists.

Acceptance of self-defense pleas is not universal. In Birmingham, Ala., Hazel Kontos was convicted and sentenced to life in prison in December 1977 for shooting her husband despite her contention that he had slapped her around and once held

---

[16] Elizabeth M. Schneider and Susan B. Jordan, "Representation of Women Who Defend Themselves In Response to Physical or Sexual Assault," Center for Constitutional Rights, 1978.
[17] Quoted in *The New York Times*, March 10, 1978.

her at gunpoint. In Waupaca, Wis., Jennifer Patri, a Sunday school teacher and PTA president, was convicted and sentenced to 10 years in prison for the shooting death of her auto-repairman husband. Patri had pleaded self-defense. Her lawyer argued that her husband beat and sexually abused her and that he also molested their 12-year-old daughter. Like many battered women, Patri said she had never called the police for help because of feelings of shame.

Generational Theory of Violence

WHAT MAKES someone physically abuse their children or their spouse? No one knows for sure, but recent studies seem to confirm the long-held belief that children who witness violent acts between their parents or who are victims of parental violence themselves often grow up to become the wife abusers and child abusers of their generation. "Family violence is usually a learned pattern of behavior," according to psychologist B.L. Daley. "Often the behavior is modeled on the father or other adult male figures. The mother also contributes by accepting this behavior."[18]

A 1975 British study of 100 abusive husbands indicated that over half of them had witnessed their fathers battering their mothers.[19] A 1975 study by John D. Flynn of Western Michigan University on spouse abuse in the area around Kalamazoo, Mich., indicated that two-fifths of the wife beaters studied had been abused as children.[20] A study by D.G. Gil, author of *Violence Against Children: Physical Child Abuse in the United States* (1970), found that 14 percent of the abusive mothers studied and 7 percent of the abusive fathers had been abused as children.

"The chances of a battered child becoming a battering adult are very, very strong," said sociologist Suzanne K. Steinmetz. "I found that there were patterns that extended over three generations. So that if you had a grandmother and a grandfather who perhaps screamed and yelled at each other and maybe occasionally slapped each other, they tended to use those methods on their children, and their children tended to use those methods

---

[18] Quoted by Roger Langley and Richard C. Levy in *Wife Beating: The Silent Crisis* (1977), p. 50.

[19] J.J. Gayford, "Wife Battering: A Preliminary Survey of 100 Cases," *British Medical Journal*, Jan. 25, 1977, pp. 194-197.

[20] John D. Flynn, "Spouse Assault: Its Dimension and Characteristics in Kalamazoo County, Michigan," Unpublished field studies in research and practice. School of Social Work, Western Michigan University, 1975.

on their brothers and sisters. And then when these children married, they tended to use the same methods on their husbands and wives and similarly on their children, and of course their children repeated it. So for three generations I found very consistent patterns on the way they resolved conflict ... the monkey see, monkey do idea."[21]

According to psychologist Lenore E. Walker, author of *The Battered Woman* (1979), children who live in homes where spouse abuse is a problem "experience the most insidious form of child abuse."

> Whether or not they are physically abused by either parent [she wrote] is less important than the psychological scars they bear from watching their fathers beat their mothers. They learn to become part of a dishonest conspiracy of silence.... Like many children who suffer from overt physical abuse, these children learn to be accommodating and cooperative. They blend into the background. They do not express anger. They do not acknowledge tension. They do expend a lot of energy avoiding problems. They live in a world of make-believe. When the screaming and yelling begin they stare transfixed but inconspicuous, watching in terror.[22]

Tolerance for Violence in Family Setting

According to Murray Straus, the norms within the family are far more accepting of physical violence than are the rules governing behavior outside the family. Straus observed that most parents are much more tolerant of physical fights among their children than they would be if their children got into a fight with someone else's child. A recent study by Straus and others found that the same children are far more violent to their own siblings than they are to other children. For example, 62 percent of the high school seniors they interviewed had hit a brother or sister during the preceding year, but "only" 35 percent had hit someone outside the family during the same year.[23]

Violence generally is tolerated in the family setting when it is labeled as discipline or punishment. "In general," Straus told the American Psychological Association last year, "the rule in the family is that if someone is doing wrong and 'won't listen to reason,' it is OK to hit. In the case of children, it is more than just OK. Most American parents see it as an obligation." A poll taken for the National Commission on the Causes and Prevention of Violence in 1969 found that the overwhelming majority of Americans (93 percent) approved of a parental spanking. About

---

[21] Quoted by Langley and Levy, *op. cit.*, p. 51.

[22] Lenore E. Walker, *The Battered Woman* (1979), pp. 149-150.

[23] Results to be included in a forthcoming book, *Violence in the American Family* by Murray Straus, Suzanne Steinmetz and Richard Gelles.

Disciplinary Measures Used by Parents

Yelled at or scolded the children	52%
Spanked them	50
Made them stay in their rooms	38
Didn't allow them to go out to play	32
Didn't let them watch television	25
Made them go to bed	23
Threatened them	15
Gave them extra chores	12
Took away their allowances	9

Source: "The General Mills American Family Report 1976-77"

20 percent of those interviewed approved of a husband slapping his wife's face in certain circumstances.[24]

After yelling and scolding, spanking still is the principal form of punishment in most families with children under 13 years of age, according to a survey conducted by Yankelovich, Skelly and White, the national market research and public opinion organization.[25] Half of the parents interviewed said they recently had spanked their children. The study found that younger parents (60 percent) were more likely to spank their children than were parents over age 35 (37 percent). Spanking also was slightly more common in families with incomes under $12,000 a year (56 percent).

Society's Mixed Views of Punishing Kids

Most parents are quick to defend their right to raise their children as they see fit. The idea of parental rights has been culturally ingrained in society from the beginning and it includes the widely accepted notion that children arc taught acceptable behavior through punishment — including physical punishment. But many psychologists and sociologists have warned that parents who use physical punishment run the risk of teaching their children that the only way to cope with stress is through the use of violence. "Violence begets violence, however peaceful and altruistic the motivation," said a 1974 study.[26]

Another study found that adults who were hit frequently as children were more likely to be violent with their mates than people who were never hit as children. "Not only does the family expose individuals to violence and techniques of violence," it said, "the family teaches approval for the use of violence."[27]

[24] See "Violence and the Media: A Staff Report to the National Commission on the Causes and Prevention of Violence," November 1969, p. 343. The National Commission on the Causes and Prevention of Violence was set up by President Johnson in 1968 after the assassinations of Sen. Robert F. Kennedy, D-N.Y., and Dr. Martin Luther King Jr.

[25] "Raising Children in a Changing Society, The General Mills American Family Report 1976-1977," p. 104.

[26] Suzanne K. Steinmetz and Murray A. Straus, eds., *Violence in the Family* (1974), p. 3.

[27] Richard Gelles, *The Violent Home* (1972), p. 171.

Seven years later, Lenore E. Walker wrote: "When we correct our children by hitting them, we teach them that it is possible to love someone and physically hurt the person at the same time, all in the name of discipline. We need to find ways of disciplining our children that do not include transmitting this message to them."[28]

The results of one of the most recent studies on the effects of physical punishment on children were published in the February 1979 issue of *Human Behavior* magazine. Sociologist Brian G. Gilmartin reported that "children who are frequently spanked tend to become highly resentful and distrustful of authority. Indeed, sometimes their often blind feelings of extreme hostility for, and distrust of, any and all authority figures reach the point of being dangerous to both themselves and others." He went on to say that "children who are often spanked tend to be conspicuously quieter, less articulate and more sullen than those who grow up under milder, more democratic forms of discipline. In addition, harshly disciplined offspring tend to display a large amount of negativity in their approach to people and to life."[29]

Evidence of a link between physical punishment and later tendencies toward violence so impressed Swedish legislators that they recently voted to outlaw spanking.[30] The new law is meant to be primarily "educational." The statute carries no penalties for spanking, but it is hoped that it will encourage children and concerned neighbors to file complaints with police or social workers. A similar ban is not likely to be enacted soon in the United States. In April 1977, for example, the U.S. Supreme Court voted 5 to 4 in favor of continuing to permit the use of corporal punishment in public schools *(Ingraham v. Wright).*

The majority held that the Eighth Amendment ban on cruel and unusual punishment "was designed to protect those convicted of crimes . . . [and] does not apply to the paddling of children as a means of maintaining discipline in public schools." Commenting on the Supreme Court's decision, Gilmartin wrote: "Banning the use of physical punishment in the schools is not going to end its use in the home. But public schools can and should be expected to set a positive example for parents to follow."

[28] Walker, *op. cit.,* p. 252.

[29] Brian G. Gilmartin, "The Case Against Spanking," *Human Behavior,* February 1979, p. 18.

[30] See *Newsweek,* April 16, 1979, p. 63.

New Efforts to Help Abusers

BREAKING the chain of violence from one generation to the next will have to involve efforts to help abusers as well as the victims of family violence. At the National Center for the Prevention of Child Abuse and Neglect in Denver, Colo., professionals directed by Dr. C. Henry Kempe[31] teach lay therapists to work in the home with abusive parents. The therapists try to help the parents become aware of their tendency to react to crises with violence. The center also operates a therapeutic day-care center for abused children, a residential treatment program for parents and children who are undergoing therapy, and a "crisis nursery" open 24 hours a day where parents can leave their children when things get tense at home.

Dr. Kempe and his colleagues have developed a screening method that may help predict which parents will abuse their children. The profile of abuse-prone parents emerged during a four-year study of 150 couples at Colorado General Hospital in Denver. Each mother was observed during labor, delivery and the post-partum period for clues that might determine how she would treat her baby. Among the things researchers were looking for was whether the mother was depressed, not affectionate with the infant, bothered by its cries, disappointed with its sex, quick to make disparaging remarks about its physical characteristics. The researchers also observed each husband, looking to see whether he was supportive and how he reacted during the delivery process.

After interviews and further observation, the mothers were divided into high- and low-risk groups. Half of the high-risk mothers were provided with intensive post-natal help and therapy; the rest received routine care. When the children were a little over two years old, 25 families in each of the three groups were randomly chosen for evaluation. The researchers found that five children in the high-risk/ordinary-care group had required hospitalization for serious injuries that were thought to have involved parental mistreatment. No such injuries were found among the children of the high-risk group that received special help or among the children of the low-risk parents.

Kempe and his colleagues insist that their study has not produced any "magic formula" for detecting parents who might be likely to harm or neglect their children. But they believe the clues they have gathered will make it easier for observant hospital personnel to spot warning signals early and try to help the

---

[31] In a paper presented to the American Academy of Pediatricians in 1961, Dr. Kempe coined the phrase "the battered child syndrome" and described the symptoms of the abnormality.

new parents adjust to their new responsibility. "Families identified early as being in need of extra parent-preparedness services must have access to intensive, continuous intervention," said one of the researchers, Dr. Jane Gray. "It makes little sense to provide excellent prenatal, obstetric and neonatal care only to abandon the most needy young families at the hospital door and leave the child rearing to chance."[32]

The National Center on Child Abuse and Neglect has observed that "even if it is possible to identify successfully a high-risk group of parents, the next step, intervention, is by no means easy. Ethical and legal problems involving the rights of parents to privacy versus the rights of children, and the states' right to intervene if parents object, are not easily solved. There is an additional concern about labeling these parents 'potential abusers' and the possibility that this can become a self-fulfilling prophecy."[33]

Preventing Abuse and Treating Abusers

Many people think the best cure for child abuse is a dose of prevention in the form of training for parents. "It's ironic that the most important job many of us will ever do is one for which most of us receive absolutely no training," Kitty Ward of the Massachusetts Society for the Prevention of Cruelty to Children said in 1977.[34] Studies have found that abusive parents often lack specific knowledge of what children do at various stages of their development and therefore have unrealistic expectations for their children. When the children fail to meet these expectations, the parents often erupt in violence.

Many experts think child care should become a required part of the curriculum in high schools. Education for Parenthood, a program sponsored by the Department of Health, Education and Welfare, attempts to teach students the "joys and responsibilities" of being a parent. The course currently is being given to approximately 121,000 high school students across the country.

One of the most successful treatment methods for abusive parents was started in 1970 by a California mother who prefers to be known as Jolly K. She is a former abusive parent who in one instance threw a kitchen knife at her six-year-old daughter and in another tried to strangle her. When Jolly could find no agency providing the kind of help she wanted, she founded her own and called it Mothers Anonymous. Known today as Parents

[32] Quoted in *Human Behavior*, May 1978, p. 67. See also Jane Gray et al., "Perinatal Assessment of Mother-Baby Interaction," in *Child Abuse and Neglect: The Family and the Community* (1976) edited by R.E. Helfer and C. Henry Kempe.

[33] National Center on Child Abuse and Neglect: "1977 Analysis of Child Abuse and Neglect Research," January 1978, p. 22.

[34] Quoted in *Newsweek*, Oct. 10, 1977, p. 115.

Anonymous, the organization claims to have over 500 chapters in the United States and Canada. Patterned after Alcoholics Anonymous, the group gives parents an opportunity to meet each other and share their problems. "Child abusers are going through hell," Jolly K. said in an interview in 1975. "We have a vision of how powerful our anger can be, a concept of where this anger will take us if we are pushed too far, and the constant dread that we will be pushed that far."[35]

Besides giving psychological support to each other at meetings, members of Parents Anonymous also contact one another by telephone when a crisis develops at home. Emergency "hot lines" are sponsored by many groups interested in helping abusive parents. A survey conducted by the National Center on Child Abuse and Neglect in 1978 found child abuse hot lines in at least 52 communities across the country.[36] According to the center, hot lines "provide isolated parents with a sympathetic, concerned individual who will listen as the caller airs frustrations, vents anger (which might otherwise have been directed at the children), or simply expresses feelings which cannot be confided to friends or relatives."

Besides the emergency hot lines serving the needs of anxiety-ridden parents, there also are a growing number of telephone lines set up to encourage neighbors, relatives, social workers and others to report suspected cases of child abuse. The National Center on Child Abuse and Neglect reports that at least 10 states — Arkansas, Colorado, Iowa, Mississippi, Missouri, New Jersey, New York, Pennsylvania, Virginia and West Virginia — have established these child abuse reporting lines through legislation. Hot line services also are being made available to spouse abusers, according to a recent survey by the Center for Women Policy Studies.[37]

Special Aid Programs for Wife Batterers

A 24-hour-a-day hot line is run by the Victims Information Bureau of Suffolk Inc. (VIBS) in Hauppauge, N.Y. "The majority of women coming to VIBS want to remain in their marriages, but without the violence," said Executive Director James Walsh. "We believe that battering will not stop unless both partners are involved in counseling. The emphasis . . . is on restructuring relationships. . . ."

In its survey, the Center for Women Policy Studies found

---

[35] Quoted by Judith Reed in "Working with Abusive Parents; A Parent's View," *Children Today*, May-June 1975, p. 6.

[36] National Center on Child Abuse and Neglect, "Child Abuse and Neglect Helplines," August 1978.

[37] See the October 1978 issue of *Response*, a newsletter published by the Center for Women Policy Studies.

several programs that work exclusively with abusive men. One is EMERGE in Somerville, Mass. It grew out of the concern of women working in local shelters who saw the need for such a service. The program emphasizes that "it is important for men to begin to talk about battering — why it starts, what leads to it, how it affects individuals and relationships, and what can be done to stop it." To encourage this, EMERGE provides "a safe environment for men to explore the roots of their violence and to learn ways to change their behavior."

Another program concerned directly with the abuser is Therapy for Abusive Behavior (TAB) in Baltimore, Md. The program is run by three women volunteers with the assistance and cooperation of the Southern Baltimore Police District commander and one of his community relations officers. It was started to give abusers the "opportunity for self-help in the areas of personal growth and development by actively participating in a program designed to identify and change violent behavior patterns." TAB teaches men more effective techniques for handling situations and relationships, while it provides a supportive network for the men during and after the program.

According to the Center for Women Policy Studies, the TAB program "is unique in that it intervenes to help the abuser at the initial stages of his contact with the courts. . . . Instead of allowing the litigation to continue, a judge may place the abuser in the TAB program, under the condition that he attend the program regularly or else re-enter the judicial system."

Minneapolis, Minn., has several programs to help spouse abusers. These include the Citizens' Dispute Settlement Project, the Walk-in Counseling Center, the Twin Cities Men's Center and men's groups within the state's Family and Children's Services department. Other efforts to help spouse abusers have been established in Seattle, Wash., Portland, Ore., and Pittsburgh, Pa. The relatively small number of programs operating to help abusive husbands is perhaps an indication of the reluctance of many men to seek help. "It must be understood that the husband is caught by the same societal values as his wife," explained James Walsh of the VIBS program. "He has been taught that men are not supposed to express feelings and that he must handle his own problems and not ask for help."

Therapy Techniques for Troubled Couples

If the husband is willing to undergo treatment or counseling, successful changes in his behavior can be accomplished in up to 80 percent of the cases, according to Sanford Sherman, executive director of Jewish Family Services in New York.[38] Sherman

[38] Quoted in Langley and Levy, *op. cit.*, p. 201.

recommends having the husband and wife visit the therapist together. "It's important for both partners to understand that [the husband is] afraid. He fears loss of status, loss of life, and paradoxically, loss of his wife. The fear is intolerable to him. He must choose either fight or flight. With a vulnerable woman present, the tendency is to fight." Sherman said the man must be taught non-violent ways of behaving when he is enraged, to get him to translate his anger into words or to take it out on objects rather than people.

The assumption that most men will stop their abusive behavior if they participate in therapy is not universally accepted. Among those who disagree is Lenore E. Walker. "Very few traditional techniques of couples therapy apply to battering couples," she wrote. "Many of these methods include teaching couples how to fight fairer and better. . . . Battering couples do not need to learn new fighting behavior. Rather, they need to learn to control their anger."[39]

Another problem with traditional couples therapy, Walker said, is that its primary goal is to make the relationship better. "With battering couples, the survival of the relationship [should be] secondary. The goal is to strengthen each individual to be able to build a new, healthier relationship. Success is achieved if the individuals are strengthened, even if the relationship itself is not able to survive." Walker and her late husband, Dr. Morton Flax, a psychologist, developed a technique which, she said, "has been successful in limiting the severity of battering incidents, although it has not yet eliminated battering incidents completely." Most couples in a battering relationship have extremely poor communications skills. "Their verbal and non-verbal communication is fraught with distortion and misinterpretation. . . ," Walker said. "We begin by teaching the couple a signal to use with each other when either one begins to feel tension rising. . . . Often it takes a lot of work to teach the couples to recognize their own cues. Once they learn to feel their tension at minimum levels, we can begin to prevent the tension build-up that causes an acute battering incident."

Dr. Walker admitted that this type of therapy is "time-consuming, expensive and exhausting for both the couple and the therapists." And while it may help the two parties involved, therapy does little to address the broader problem of violence in the family. Both spouse abuse and child abuse are symptomatic of deep, underlying stress within the family. Until the dynamics of the problem are better understood, more support systems must be provided the growing number of victims of domestic violence.

[39] Walker, *op. cit.*, p. 245.

Selected Bibliography

Books

Gelles, Richard J., *The Violent Home: A Study of Physical Aggression Between Husbands and Wives,* Sage Publications, 1972.

Langley, Roger and Richard C. Levy, *Wife Beating: The Silent Crisis,* E.P. Dutton, 1977.

Martin, Del, *Battered Wives,* Glide Publications, 1976.

Pizzey, Erin, *Scream Quietly or the Neighbors Will Hear,* Anchor Press, 1974.

Steinmetz, Suzanne K. and Murray A. Straus, eds., *Violence in the Family,* Harper & Row, 1974.

Walker, Lenore E., *The Battered Woman,* Harper & Row, 1979.

Walters, David R., *Physical and Sexual Abuse of Children: Causes and Treatment,* Indiana University Press, 1975.

Articles

"Authorities Face Up to the Child Abuse Problem," *U.S. News & World Report,* May 3, 1976.

Eisenberg, Susan and Patricia Micklow, "The Assaulted Wife: 'Catch 22' Revisited," *Women's Rights Law Reporter,* spring-summer 1977.

Fields, Marjory D., "Wife Beating: the Hidden Offense," *New York Law Journal,* April 29, 1976.

Franke, Linda Bird, "Battered Women," *Newsweek,* Feb. 2, 1976.

Gelles, Richard J., "Abused Wives: Why Do They Stay," *Journal of Marriage and the Family,* November 1976.

Gingold, Judith, "One of these days — Pow — right in the kisser," *Ms.,* August 1976.

Jacobson, Beverly, "Battered Women," *Civil Rights Digest,* summer 1977.

Potter, Joan, "Police and the Battered Wife: The Search for Understanding," *Police Magazine,* September 1978.

Shiels, Merrill, "The Battered Children," *Newsweek,* Oct. 10, 1977.

Straus, Murray A., "Wife Beating: How Common and Why?" *Victimology,* November 1977.

"The Battered Husbands," *Time,* March 20, 1978.

Reports and Studies

"Battered Women: Issues of Public Policy," A Consultation Sponsored by the U.S. Commission on Civil Rights, Washington, D.C., Jan. 30-31, 1978.

Editorial Research Reports: "Child Abuse," 1976 Vol. I, pp. 65-84; "The Changing American Family," 1977 Vol. I, pp. 413-432.

National Center on Child Abuse and Neglect, "1977 Analysis of Child Abuse and Neglect Research," January 1978.

Schneider, Elizabeth M. and Susan B. Jordan, "Representation of Women Who Defend Themselves In Response to Physical or Sexual Assault," Center for Constitutional Rights, 1978.

Straus, Murray A., Suzanne K. Steinmetz and Richard J. Gelles, "Violence in the Family: An Assessment of Knowledge and Needs," paper presented to the American Association for the Advancement of Science, Feb. 23, 1976.

INDEX